Winner of *Le Prix Adolphe Bentinck* for 1982
for the work that best contributes
to the unity and cause of peace in Europe

Duties Beyond Borders

THE FRANK W. ABRAMS LECTURES

Duties Beyond Borders

On the Limits and Possibilities of
Ethical International Politics

STANLEY HOFFMANN

SYRACUSE UNIVERSITY PRESS

Copyright © 1981 by Syracuse University Press
Syracuse, New York 13244-5160

First published 1981
All Rights Reserved

First Edition
95 94 93 92 91 90 89 88   12 11 10 9 8

Library of Congress Cataloguing in Publication Data

Hoffmann, Stanley.
Duties Beyond Borders.

Includes bibliographical references and index.
1. International relations. 2. International relations—
Moral and religious aspects. I. Title.
JX1255.H56   327.1'01   81-2401
ISBN 0-8156-0167-0   AACR2
ISBN 0-8156-0168-9 (pbk.)

Manufactured in the United States of America

To DITA SHKLAR—
formidable colleague,
and a friend for all seasons

STANLEY HOFFMANN received degrees from Paris Law School, Institut d'Études Politiques, and Harvard University and is the author of *Primacy or World Order* and *Decline or Renewal? France since the 1930s.* He is Chairman of the Center for European Studies and Douglas Dillon Professor of the Civilization of France, Harvard University.

Contents

Foreword

$\mathcal{T}$HE ABRAMS LECTURE SERIES is financed by a grant from the Exxon Education Foundation in memory of the late Frank W. Abrams, former chairman of the board of the Standard Oil Company (New Jersey), the predecessor of Exxon, and former chairman of the board of trustees of Syracuse University.

A member of Syracuse University's Class of 1912, Mr. Abrams was a life-long leader in support of higher education. He was a founder of the Council for Financial Aid to Education, chairman of the Ford Foundation's Fund for the Advancement of Education, and a trustee for the Alfred E. Sloan Foundation.

Mr. Abrams was one of the key pioneers who awakened American business, both through education and landmark legal precedents, to the need for financial support by business for private higher education. It was a contribution by Mr. Abrams, the importance of which cannot be overemphasized, which makes it particularly appropriate that this lecture series be presented in his name.

The 1980 lecture series by Stanley Hoffmann, which initiated this undertaking by Syracuse University and the Exxon Education Foundation, came at a time of intellectual ferment on the Syracuse campus. It is clear that the series has added a new and substantial component to the richness of academic life at the University.

Melvin A. Eggers
Chancellor
Syracuse University

Preface

*T*HE ESSAYS which follow are based on five lectures that I gave, between February and April 1980, at Syracuse University, as the first Frank W. Abrams lecturer. I have tried to preserve as much as possible the somewhat informal and relaxed tone of a lecture series. I believe that the issues discussed here, while susceptible to highly sophisticated and learned treatment, are important enough, and frequently misconceived enough, to deserve a somewhat broader approach. At the risk of losing fine points, qualifications, exceptions, and precision, I have chosen to be sketchy and a bit didactic, in the hope that the main lines of the discussion will be clear, if not convincing to all.

My main concern has been to try to show that there are ways—narrow to be sure—to reconcile what is usually referred to as the realistic approach to international politics, with the demands of morality. Neither these demands nor the "game of states"—their quest for power, their search for unilateral advantages, their rivalry, their insecurity—will go away. The brand of realism that declares moral behavior in international affairs impossible, or assigns to states a special morality profoundly different from that of individuals or of groups within the state, may have much of history on its side. And yet the claims of ordinary morality, the clamor for a kind of state conduct that does not almost inevitably lead to deceit and violence, cannot be suppressed. We must remember that states are led by human beings whose actions affect human beings within and outside: considerations of good and evil, right or wrong are therefore both inevitable and legitimate. But we cannot indulge in flings of moralism that assume that the problem to be addressed—can there be moral behavior in a world of states—has already been solved by the demise of the states, or that traditional state behavior will be transformed by indignation and exhortation alone. An attempt at reconciliation such as this acknowledges the constraints of international politics, the realities of competition in uncertainty, and yet it aims at changing quite thoroughly the traditional rules of the game. Such an effort will undoubtedly be deemed naive by the "realists" and timid by the utopians. So be it.

A second concern is a precondition for the reconciliation between ethics and international politics: overcoming the distinction, so fundamental to foreign policy, between "us" and "them," nationals and foreigners. We all have in our minds the image (often an embellishment of reality) of the nation as a community whose members are bound by ties of solidarity far stronger than the ties of mutual interest, and lasting even when the latter do not exist. Moral feelings, a sense of ethical obligation, derive from these bonds. Community is what makes altruistic individual behavior, or enlightened group behavior, possible. In the absence of any international community, however, transnational ties are far weaker: they derive merely from concerns of reciprocity and complementarity, that is, from considerations of interest and fear, and they tend to exist only among states, rather than among individuals regardless of borders. It is in order to safeguard the national community from outside or internal threats that statesmen are, often, granted the right to behave in a way that would be deemed evil for individuals or groups within the state. Indeed, it is partly because of the ideal of common participation in the general will of a free nation that restraints have gradually been imposed on the domestic powers of governments—that governments have acknowledged an obligation to deal with people as citizens not subjects. But there is no global general will, and no worldwide ethical agreement on restraints governments should observe toward other states and strangers abroad. We cannot ignore this essential distinction. And yet, unless we lower the barrier, and move toward the acceptance of restraints and of positive obligations beyond the borders, the world is doomed to remain a jungle, and the arrangements of international law will be no more than temporary artifices.

A third concern has been to try to find a path that can be travelled by believers in different moral codes, even though it is clearly traced by a partisan of a liberal one. There is probably no way in which the din of conflicting moralities can lead to perfect harmony, and there is surely no way of accommodating all moral claims—not only because they are incompatible, but also because to consider them all valid would be an abdication of moral judgment. What follows will therefore displease or disappoint those who are not of my own persuasion. But the moral problem in international affairs consists precisely in trying to organize a reasonably peaceful coexistence of antagonistic claims. A world in which such coexistence prevails, and where only those claims that threaten the survival of peoples and states are squashed, is the only one in which a chance for moral foreign policy behavior exists.

I want to thank Chancellor Melvin A. Eggers and Dean Guthrie Birkhead for having given me this opportunity to worry about problems that the students of international relations find on their way, but all too rarely confront directly. I wish also to thank the Chancellor's Assistant, James Geis, whose kind and efficient support has been invaluable. Also, I express my gratitude to my friend and colleague Joseph Nye, and to my students Theodore Koontz and Michael Smith, whose detailed comments and criticisms have been challenging and helpful.

SH

Duties Beyond Borders

Down the road, it is then possible to visualize a kind of social science that would be very different from the one most of us have been practicing: a moral-social science where moral considerations are not repressed or kept apart, but are systematically commingled with analytic argument, without guilt feelings over any lack of integration; where the transition from preaching to proving and back again is performed frequently and with ease; and where moral considerations need no longer be smuggled in surreptitiously, nor expressed unconsciously, but are displayed openly and disarmingly.

Albert O. Hirschman

Ethics and International Affairs

PRELIMINARIES

*T*HE PROBLEMS that will be examined in these essays
could be defined in a number of ways. For instance:
What is the proper place of ethical concerns, imperatives,
or restraints in international affairs? In other words,
where, if at all, do norms for moral behavior, considerations of right and wrong fit in the relations between
states? Given the world as it is, what would be a morally
acceptable international milieu, and how can one achieve
it? What are the consequences of introducing explicitly
moral considerations into the affairs of states? I will try to
deal briefly with these questions in the following manner.

I will discuss them as a political scientist, not as a
philosopher, for a number of reasons. The first and best
Napoleon would have said to stop after that first) is that I
am not a philosopher. My training is not in philosophy, or
in moral philosophy; it is in history, and in political science and law. My interest is that of a student of those
fields, and of a citizen. Also, my concern is less with what
should be done, although I am, as we shall see, deeply
interested in that, than with *how* one can get to what
should be done. A comparison between what I will try to
say and what has been written recently, and eloquently, by
my friend and former colleague Michael Walzer in his
book on *Just and Unjust Wars*[1] may be of help. His line
goes from a scrutiny of existing or generally accepted

1

norms, to his view of the "ought," to the "is." His business is, properly, applied ethics; he tries to define what ought to be the just causes of war, or the right way of fighting them, and he compares his standards with the (usually somber) realities of warfare. My way is the opposite, starting from what is and groping toward the "ought": it is an attempt at uplifting politics. To be sure, uplifted politics and applied ethics ought to converge; and I hope that we will meet halfway, although without having necessarily chosen our rendezvous for the same reasons.

Secondly, I am attempting not to reach exclusively specialists and scholars who have dealt professionally with these questions, but also people outside the scholarly world. This means that I shall examine these issues in as practical and common-sensical a way as possible. My last reason for not wanting to invade philosophy is that when philosophers deal with the ethics of politics the results are not always, in my opinion, very satisfying. Some of the purely theoretical discussions about ethics in world affairs leave me puzzled. At present, for instance, there is a debate about the application of John Rawls's theory of justice to international relations. It is very fascinating, but it has very little relevance to reality, for two reasons. In his learned and massive tome, Rawls asks what would happen if individuals met under what he calls a "veil of ignorance," in a hypothetical "original position" in which they do not know who they are—they know nothing about their respective situations, fortunes, or conceptions—in order to try to agree on principles of justice, on the assignment of rights and duties, on the distribution of benefits and costs, while furthering their own interests. When one asks what would happen if, instead of having individuals meeting under those conditions, each one representing only himself, we had representatives of nations meeting behind that "veil of ignorance" in order to choose the principles of international justice, there are fundamental differences between various authors (one of whom is Rawls). Some of them even say that Rawls is perfectly wrong in describing what, in his opinion, they would decide if they were representatives of nations. Thus we have already a debate on the very nature of the principles of justice in world affairs: are they principles of *interstate* justice, or principles of *universal* justice? In domestic affairs, we agree that the problem is one of justice for individuals (if we don't, the whole Rawlsian construction collapses). In international politics we shall again and again come across the "state vs. human beings" or "nation vs. individuals" problem, an old bone of contention for students of international law.

But there is another reason for being suspicious of that exercise. It is not only intellectually but politically very exciting to ask oneself, as Rawls does, what should be the perfect fair society. For the whole enterprise is based on two conditions that give it practical relevance—that make of the principles derived by Rawls criteria for judging existing societies and guidelines for changing them—but that are missing in the international milieu. First, the original position, for all its hypothetical character, corresponds not only to the old notion of the state of nature, but above all to the fundamental postulate of democratic government, "equality between human beings as moral persons"[2]: the principles of justice are derived from a procedure of equalitarian democratic participation, which resembles the political framework of a number of (predominantly Western) nations. Rawls describes himself as the heir not of all social contract theory, but of that of Locke, Rousseau, and Kant— certainly not that of Hobbes, in which the individuals abdicate to the Leviathan they have set up. Now, whereas citizens in democratic states resemble the individuals in Rawls's state of nature, there is no resemblance at all between state representatives supposedly meeting in

Rawls's original position, and the reality of international affairs. To be sure, in real domestic life there are huge inequalities in status and wealth, even in democracies, and in international life, conversely, there is the legal principle of state equality. But the dynamics are quite different: constitutional democracy is based on the principle of equal participation, to which even the rich and the well-born pay lip service (and whose application makes the erosion of at least some of the inequalities of status and wealth possible). In world affairs, the principle of state equality is accepted as a formal norm, not as a substantive one. International politics severely restricts its operational consequences and remains dominated by the interplay of might and wealth—it is the big powers who tend to lay down the law.

The second difference lies in the realm of enforcement. The kinds of principles of justice which Rawls thinks people in his state of nature would arrive at make sense as long as all those individuals can establish a state which would have, as all states do, a legitimate monopoly of constraint; so that the individuals, having agreed on certain principles, would be obliged to stick to them: the state could enforce them. And in fact the state often tries to approximate the standards of justice at which these individuals are supposed to have arrived. This exercise is practically meaningless in the international milieu, because even if state representatives did agree, behind the "veil of ignorance," on standards of international justice, in a milieu where self-help is the rule and where force can always be used by each agent, there is no guarantee whatsoever that those principles would ever stick for very long.

In other words, when you are dealing with a domestic order, the gap between what Rawls calls the "original position" and reality is often no more than a normative gap—if you prefer, an inspiration. The principles at which people would arrive in that original position indicate a direction in which the society and the state ought to go and are, in many instances, politically (if not economically) equipped to go. In international affairs, even if one could agree on what those norms should be, the goal remains utopian—a mirage: there is no way of obliging, say, those states that would find the application of the principles intolerable to respect them. Unless Rawls is right about the principles that representatives of nations would arrive at (he lists them in a couple of pages), they amount to an exercise in pure formalism, which is not very interesting. I shall therefore proceed not from that fragile original position, but from political realities.

The topics that will be discussed are the following. First, I shall examine what could be called the moral problem itself: Can there be moral behavior in international affairs? And if so, under what conditions? Then I will turn to three of the most burning contemporary issues. The first one is the case of moral restraints on the use of force. This used to be at the core of moral theories of foreign policy behavior, many centuries ago. It has become a most essential problem again in the twentieth century. We have had two savage world wars. In recent years the United States has gone through a fierce debate over Vietnam, which raised many questions. Did we have the right to intervene? This question provoked not one debate, but two—a debate on our ends, of course, but also a debate on the nature of the conflict. What kind of war was it? Was it a civil war, or was it an international struggle? There was a further question: Did we fight well? Hence a debate on the means. And, last but not least, what were the moral effects of the outcome—in other words, a debate on the consequences also.

The second case is the formidable and tormenting issue of human rights. Is this a proper concern for foreign policy at all? If it is, with what rights should one be concerned? How important is the promotion of these rights in the overall hierarchy of objectives which a state must have? What are the tradeoffs, and also what means is it wise to use if one decides to promote such rights?

Third, I will examine the problems of distibutive justice, about which there begins to be an enormous literature that raises very interesting questions. Are there obligations between rich and poor nations comparable to those which most domestic societies accept toward the poorer members of those societies? If there are such obligations, what is their destination? Are they owed to governments? Or to individuals in those poorer countries? For what purposes? At what costs to oneself?

Finally, I shall try to discuss what a morally livable world order would look like, given the world as it is—and it is cacaphonic in any dimension you want to look at—in the horizontal dimension (the relations between the major powers), in the vertical dimension (the relations between the weak and the strong), and in what could be called the functional dimension, since world politics these days is a number of different games played with very different means, not always by the same actors. In each instance my objective is to review, as unobtrusively and unpedantically as possible, the literature on the subject in order to describe the main (and frequently incompatible) positions; also, I shall try to navigate between the extremes (except in the rare cases where I might agree with one) and suggest my own position.

Another remark about these essays: the problems of international relations exist at different levels. For obvious reasons—this is not supposed to be an encyclopedia—I will concern myself mainly with one. At least three layers can be distinguished; first of all, there are the moral dilemmas of the statesmen, of the decision makers. Then we find the moral choices of those who carry out those decisions, mainly, to use broad categories, the diplomats and the soldiers. Finally, there comes the rest of us (some may want to treat intellectuals as a separate category altogether). I will emphasize primarily the first level, the problems of the statesmen. Theirs is the burden of putting burdens on everyone else. But it will be useful to cast a glance at the other levels also. For when we think about those who carry out the decisions, whether it is the diplomats and the soldiers or the rest of us, we encounter in the domain of foreign policy a special case of the general problems of the obligations of citizenship. What are one's rights or one's duties toward the state? The average citizen would have no problem, dilemma, agony, or choice caused by the acts of his state in foreign affairs if we took one of two positions, neither of which I recommend. One would be that each citizen has an absolute duty to obey the government. This would eliminate the moral problem of citizenship altogether. There is a second way of eliminating the problem: by making the following distinction. One could argue that indeed we all have rights as well as duties toward our government in domestic affairs—there is no such thing as "Right or wrong, my government" in such matters. But there is such a thing as "Right or wrong, my country." In other words, one could take the position that whereas there is no obligation that covers the whole political field, there is a duty of obedience limited to foreign policy, either because one believes that foreign policy does not raise moral problems anyhow, or because one believes that the moral issues of foreign policy are properly the preserve of the government, which one should obey, given the nature of the competition among states (both its complexities, which require expertise, and its intensity, which demands untroubled steering). This is not my position, as will become clear below.

If, therefore, there are serious citizenship problems, two very interesting questions arise, with which I will not deal fully, but which we should remember. What should be the behavior of the citizens in general, and particularly of the soldiers and diplomats, and of the intellectuals, when their government engages in an immoral foreign policy? This was, of course, an extraordinarily vital and difficult problem for German citizens and for German officials in the Nazi period. The other question, which is quite different, is for the citizens or the civil servants or the soldiers of a domestically oppressive state, whether it acts badly abroad or not. How should these citizens behave toward the outside world? Should they call for help? Or should they essentially do their job by themselves, throw out the tyrants themselves, and keep the outside world at arms' length? These are not simple questions.

Finally, before reaching the subject itself, it is always good for the author to put his cards on the table. Since all attempts at discussing moral issues in domestic or international affairs are necessarily colored by the biases of the writer, let me describe my own as simply as possible. I consider myself to be one of those old-fashioned and increasingly dinosaur-like types, a liberal. There must be a few of us left. I don't apologize for it. Indeed, I feel sorry for those who aren't. (I realize that this constitutes the majority of mankind). Inevitably this will be reflected here. I am neither a Marxist nor a conservative, nor a neo-Marxist nor a neo-conservative. To be a liberal does not mean necessarily to believe in progress, it means only to believe in a (limited and reversible) perfectibility of man and society, and particularly in the possibility of devising institutions, based on consent, that will make society more humane and more just, and the citizens' lot better. This means—conservatives would agree—that the state should be servant of society, not the other way around, but also that this servant's role is vital and can be salutary. And it means—Marxists would agree—that injustices that are the patterned products of economic systems, social stratification, or ethnic biases must be fought; but also that no philosophy of history provides us once and for all with a tool kit or a destination. As a liberal I do believe that questions about morality—including the morality of foreign policy decisions—are questions about the rights and duties, as well as about the happiness and burdens, of individuals. This does not mean that I deny the importance of groups—kinship groups, ethnic groups, classes, nations; obviously, it is in and through them that individuals act and fulfill themselves (most of the time—sometimes they fulfill themselves by reacting against these groupings). But these are made of individuals, and, in my view, their own rights and duties derive from the role they play at the service of their members (a service that can indeed require sacrifices on the part of the individuals, insofar as the life, happiness, and opportunities of persons depend on the groups, and especially on the nations', own existence, freedom, and prosperity). Individuals receive their first moral notions from the groups in which they live and continue to receive moral dictates from them throughout their lives. But this does not mean that there can be *no* moral development outside the groups. We have in ourselves a moral faculty that is awakened and sharpened by our relations with others, but which, once it is aroused, can grow and evolve apart from group pressures or commands. The group, therefore, while always a trigger, and often a help, can become an oppressive obstacle. Moral education consists precisely in helping the individual both realize what he owes the group and emancipate himself from group bondage.

Also as a liberal, my position is reformist or meliorist, not revolutionary. This does not mean that I believe revolutions to be necessarily evil, or even avoidable. They are often inevitable, and sometimes beneficial, given the alternatives. But it means that I am addicted to the search for a better, less destructive, more tolerant alternative to an unbearable or nefarious status quo—an alternative more respectful of the rights or of the humanity of opponents.

Thus it is a liberal's view of morality in international affairs that will be found here, whenever I deal with *oughts*. Moreover, one is always shaped by one's own experiences; my formative experience was in the thirties and World War II, particularly the years when the Nazi stain spread over Europe, and when the Nazis occupied France. This has kept me with a lifelong, perverse preoccupation with world wars; and again, to make my biases very clear, I do not like them. So while I am not a pacifist, Christian or otherwise—the experience of the Thirties, so perfectly distilled in Ionesco's *Rhinoceros,* rules this out—I have a very strong belief that no war is very often better than war (indeed, a world war was avoidable as late as September 1938). It would be a mistake to make you believe that I have for actual, real-life military battles the enthusiasm that some of my friends and colleagues seem to feel.

THE MORAL PROBLEM
IN INTERNATIONAL RELATIONS

Two central questions have been discussed for a long time. First, is there a possibility of moral choice for statesmen in international relations? And secondly, if one assumes that there is, what are the limits of moral choice? On the first question, nobody has ever argued that there *should* be no choice, but many people have asserted that there *can* be none. What are their arguments, and how valid are they? There are two kinds of arguments. The most radical remains that of Hobbes: Nations are in a state of nature (indeed it is that state which suggests what the individual's pre-Leviathan state of nature must look like). It is a state of anarchy, conflicting desires, and scarcity. There is a general struggle for power, fueled by what he calls "competition," "diffidence," and "glory." In this competition the only universal concern is survival. Gresham's law operates: even those who would like to pursue loftier goals cannot escape from the contest waged by the power greedy. This means that the right of nature is the liberty to use one's power of self-preservation, and that the laws of nature are simply laws of self-preservation, dictated by reason; and those laws involve both self-defense and war. In such a state there is no morality; in fact, morality is simply the name given to behavior in conformity with the law of an established domestic order—with the positive legislation of a Leviathan in which the enforcement of humane laws of self-preservation becomes possible. But in international affairs, which is a state of nature, and in which there is no such Leviathan, there can be no morality. It is a definitional problem.

This means that international affairs remain the domain so well described by probably the most famous text of history, Thucydides' Melian dialog between the Athenians and the Melians. The Athenians tell the Melians that in international affairs the strong do what they can and the weak do what they must, and that, anyhow, discussion of rights is valid only among equals. The Melians insist on talking about right and justice. The Athenians reply "that expediency goes with security, while justice and honor cannot be followed without danger,"[3] and they conquer and kill the Melians. This approach to the problem is what Robert W. Tucker calls, euphemistically, a "naturalistic" conception.[4] It means that international relations is the domain of necessity, in which the only ends, which are dictated by the nature of the game, are security and survival. On behalf of those ends any means can be used. This is literally a structural explanation; it starts from the nature of international politics, and everything derives from it mechanistically and logically.

There is another, very similar, argument, not perhaps the most radical—the Hobbesian is the most radical—but the most tragic, and that is the view of Max Weber.[5] It is not mechanistic; it is philosophical. It is not, as in the case of Hobbes, naturalistic and sardonic. It is, as usual with Max Weber, depressed and tormented. It starts with his famous opposition between the ethics of conviction, the ethics of the saints or of the prophets, the ethics of ultimate ends, and the ethics of responsibility, which is the ethics of all politics, domestic or foreign. The point he makes, which is not exactly new with him, is that the ethics of responsibility, the ethics of political action always inevitably entails the use of evil means. But he goes beyond this, for he stresses that this need to resort to evil means is by far at its greatest, and inevitably so, in international affairs, because the world scene, by contrast with domestic politics, is the domain of inexpiable, irreconcilable, *and* violent conflicts of values, represented by the states. All politics entails conflict. But the states are the ultimate, supreme expression of the values locked in a struggle for existence and supremacy. There is nothing above them, and they are armed. It is an interesting blend of Hegel, whose agonistic philosophy Weber had of course absorbed, and of a kind of Darwinian-Nietzschean view of the international competition. And it is a very stark view, in two different ways: first of all, it assumes that for people who believe in an ethics of responsibility, which means, of course, the statesmen, the power of the nation-state must be their supreme value, *by definition.* If anybody had a concern other than the power of the state as his supreme value, he would be out of the sphere of political action. The political sphere is by definition that in which there is nothing above the nation. That is stark enough. What makes it even starker is that he not only says this, but he also subordinates domestic politics and economic policy to it. Domestic politics must be tailored to and corseted by this supreme value. In other words, he does not only eliminate moral choice about ends outside; he does not only present international politics as the domain of uncompromising moral conflicts. Because of this, he also very sharply wants to limit moral choice within. Moral choice tends to be relegated to the realm of means—and even there it is limited since Weber calls violence the decisive means in politics.

I do not believe that these arguments are convincing. Let us begin with the structural view, the Hobbesian one. Very often, there is a tendency to try to refute it by resorting to a rosier view of international relations. This alternative view is that of the secularized natural law tradition, the tradition of Grotius, of Locke, of Pufendorf. Or else, it is the antinaturalist, utilitarian conception of Hume. Both the secularized natural law thinkers and Hume start with human sociability and derive from it the existence of common norms and common interests. They argue that of course in international affairs those common norms are weak, those common interests are fragile, because there is no central power, or because a state—stronger than a mere individual in society—has less of an interest in observing them. And yet these common norms exist, and the international state of affairs is not a state of war. This is not a very convincing refutation of Hobbes, because it can easily be shown to be false, first of all by experience. We all know by experience that in many periods in history there simply are no, or very few, common norms or common interests. And it has also been very neatly demolished by Rousseau, who pointed out that in a competition, each state is above all concerned with its *own* advantage: when states calculate their interests, there is no common standard of utility.[6] Moreover, he reminds us, sociability is a force for considerable mischief, it is at the root of "amour-propre" and competition and is not necessarily a source of good behavior. In fact, sociability is to him the cause of all evils, since once we start being sociable we start comparing ourselves to one another, we start being envious, and greedy, and scheming, and violence and deception follow.

However, the stark description of international politics by Hobbes as a state of nature that is a state of (to him and in his days, bearable) war is not a perfect description of international reality either. Not at all times are states in a situation of war of all against all; it is not true throughout history, it is not true in space at any one moment. The statesman is not always knocked to the floor, having to survive or else. Also, the Hobbesian view predetermines the goal of political action by saying that it must be security and survival and nothing else, and by reducing all choices to techniques. This is patently false. Survival itself is not an unambiguous goal. Let us take three cases where survival was clearly at stake: France in 1940, Israel since its birth, Poland for the last two centuries. There were violent disagreements, not about the technique of survival but about the meaning of survival itself. Was it to be the physical survival of the French, as Pétain thought, or the "moral" survival of France, as deGaulle wanted? Is the survival of a country under foreign rule, like Poland, better served by preserving as much national spirit at home despite foreign domination, or by refusing any collaboration and keeping the flame burning abroad? Does the survival of Israel require reconciliation with the Arabs and insertion in the Middle East—Nahum Goldmann's vision—or a tough, annexationist stance—Ben Gurion's vision as long as he was in power? There are disagreements both about *what* it is that must survive, and about the time perspective. Nor is survival the only goal of states—it may be a necessary one, but when it is reasonably assured, all the other goals become manifest and come up front. If one goes back to the Melian dialog, one realizes that both the Athenians and the Melians had choices; the Melians did not have to behave like heroic self-sacrificers, and the Athenians did not have to behave like barbarians. The situation was bad enough, but the outcome was the result of choices. To paraphrase my former colleague, Mr. Brzezinski, the Melians behaved like Poles, not Czechs, and the Athenians behaved, let us say, like Nazis. This was not a necessity rising out of the structure of the game.

As for the Weberian view, it is a fallacy to assume that all statecrafts that put the power of the nation-state as the supreme value are doomed thereby to permanent conflict. It is wrong to look at the conflict of nation-states as a kind of permanent, agonizing test of fitness, to view each nation-state as a sacred, separate essence that has to be tested in battle against the others, with the outcome of the battle telling which is the morally superior essence. It is a strange nineteenth-century view, both very gloomy and very optimistic; gloomy in that it assumes that one is doomed to that kind of contest, and optimistic in assuming that after the battle is over one will play the game again as if nobody had been eliminated from it once and for all. It is also a fallacy to believe that the alleged supreme value, the power of the nation-state, is a clear-cut end. Even if one believes that the stateman has the power of the nation as his goal, and indeed must have it as a goal if he is to be a statesman, the power of the nation can be sought in very different ways, depending on the statesman's conception of power, of his nation, of the international order, and so on. A Theodore Roosevelt and a Wilson, a Bismarck and a Hitler, a Napoleon and a de Gaulle do not have the same idea of their roles. In other words, the Weberian view is both an abdication of moral judgment and a confusion of moral judgment. The answer to the first question is therefore: Yes, there is a domain of choice. But the real question then becomes how much. We must turn to the limits of moral choice. The domain is obviously extremely narrow, for three reasons mainly. The first one is a structural reason, revised in a non-Hobbesian way, but it is still the same idea: the nature of the social framework itself. The international milieu simply does not leave one much room for moral action; as Wolfers put it: "moral convictions cannot tell what roads are open to a statesman."[7] The arguments here are double. First comes one for which I have a limited amount of sympathy, for it has sometimes been carried much too far. It is the argument made at length in the writings of Reinhold Niebuhr, and briefly and much more sharply in E. H. Carr's *Twenty Years Crisis*, about the difference between individual behavior and all group behavior. Individuals can behave altruistically; for a person, "self-transcendence" is both possible and sometimes even expected, or rewarded; whereas groups in general are expected to behave selfishly; they are there literally to promote the interests of the members. If they did something else, they would betray the interests of the group. Not only is selfish behavior accepted, but one also expects of groups that they will sometimes behave in a way that would be immoral if it were indulged in by individuals. There is something in this argument, but it should not be carried too far. The notion of interest is a very tricky one; self-interest and selfishness are not identical. If all groups behaved selfishly all the time, all social life would come close to that model of enmity, of a conflict of all against all, which, as Wolfers pointed out, eliminates moral choice, but also breeds intolerable insecurity. As many pressure groups have found out—for instance die-hard business associations or revolutionary unions—purely selfish behavior, by destroying the social fabric, is not in their self-interest. Moreover, not every group interest is morally respectable; domestic society has laws that aim at deterring or punishing reprehensible group behavior. International law tries to do the same insofar as national behavior is concerned.

There is a second argument which in a way reinforces the previous one, but it exists quite independently from it, and I put more stock in it. It stresses the difference not between individuals and groups, but between individuals and groups in a domestic order on the one hand, and the statesmen on the world scene on the other. It is a two-stage argument. In the first place, in a domestic system which functions well, individuals and groups can behave morally because there is a framework of social order—in which they have a stake. *A contrario,* when that framework disappears, and survival or basic needs become the obsession of all, individuals and groups start behaving in an immoral or in a cowardly way. This is one of the points made, effectively if not totally fairly, by Marcel Ophüls' well-known movie, *The Sorrow and the Pity,* about France under Nazi occupation. When we are in an economic depression or in a civil war, we are indeed much closer to the Hobbesian floor than to the Kantian ceiling, and we behave accordingly. But in the domestic system, the statesman, being the maintainer of the framework of social order, being a man whose moral obligation is to preserve that order, will sometimes have to behave in an immoral way. This is the old Machiavellian argument: for the individual *and* the group in a well-functioning society, altruistic or enlightened behavior is possible, but the statesman's duty is to protect the general interest of the nation; and sometimes doing evil—lying, deceiving, striking out—on behalf of that interest is a necessity. De Gaulle defined the statesman, by contrast with the intellectual, as somebody who takes risks, including moral risks.

The second stage of the argument shows that this contrast between the behavior of individuals and groups in the domestic order and the statesman is particularly acute when one looks at the international milieu. Both Carr and Arnold Wolfers recognize that the statesman operating in the context of domestic politics can often behave reasonably well, even though his first duty is the maintenance of the domestic society—especially when the political system and the social order are recognized as legitimate, and of course also because of the state's monopoly of coercion. But a statesman in the international competition cannot afford moral behavior so easily; first, because of what might be called the state's duty of selfishness: as Hamilton put it, "the rule of morality... is not precisely the same between nations as between individuals. The duty of making its own welfare the guide of its own actions is much stronger upon the former than upon the latter. Existing millions and ... future generations are concerned with the present measures of a government while the consequences of the private action of an individual ordinarily terminate with himself."[8] To be sure, and as I will argue, this duty of selfishness is no license to pursue any end and to use any means, but it restricts the realm of choice. Secondly, in international relations, by contrast with domestic politics, the scope of moral conflict is infinite, whereas in a domestic order the scope is normally much more restricted. Thirdly, violence, the ever-present possibility of war, limits the range of moral opportunity. There is the state's security dilemma, there is the need to survive. And because a drastic separation between order and justice exists in international affairs, the state has to survive first;

as a statesman, you have to establish or preserve order first, and then you can worry about justice, if there is time left. International order has to be established or defended every minute, whereas domestic order is a given, and already reflects a conception of justice. In other words, the condition which drives out moral choice, or (again in Wolfers' phrase) dooms one to "out-group morality," or (in Raymond Aron's) to the morality of struggle: enmity, is much more likely to arise in international politics. And this is so because of the two fundamental differences between domestic politics and international politics: international relations is a competition of groups with no consensus among them, and with no power above them. This indeed makes for a non-Hobbesian structural argument, which explains why moral opportunities for the statesman in world affairs are quite limited.

The second reason is a philosophical argument, revised in a non-Weberian way. Even if one does not accept Weber's notion of inexpiable conflicts of values, there is, in fact, no single, operational international code of behavior. There are competing codes, rival philosophical traditions, clashing conceptions of morality. This is far worse than what went on, let us say, in the days of the just war theory. The behavior of princes was often atrocious, but at least they acknowledged a single code of legitimacy. They violated it, but they recognized it in principle. At present there are incompatible notions of legitimacy; the only common code is not an ethical one, really. The only common code, which incites both struggle and prudence, is national egoism. We behave in a certain way in Vietnam or in the Dominican Republic; the Soviets behave in a certain way in Afghanistan, the Indians "liberate" Goa, Vietnam "liberates" Cambodia. Each party denies that its acts are comparable to those of the others, and so on. It is true, as some point out, that all statesmen use the same moral language—they all argue about rights and wrongs, justice and law. And the United Nations Charter, plus a number of quasi-universal treaties, seem to provide a common grammar. Unfortunately, from the viewpoint of moral harmony, this is meaningless. A community of vocabulary is not the same thing as a community of values. When people with very different values use the same vocabulary, it debases both the vocabulary and the values hidden behind the vocabulary. This is what has been happening to notions like self-determination, non-intervention, etc. Behind the common grammar there are competing ideological logics.

Not only is there no single moral code, but there are no effective substitutes. International law and international organizations certainly are not. What limits the role of the latter is precisely the conflicts of values and interests among the members. As for international law, it is partly a fragile truce between the combatants, partly the victim of value (and of power) confrontations that have undermined many of the traditional branches of the law. World public opinion is about as fragile as the sum of conflicting domestic opinions can be—each domestic opinion being capable of oscillation, and at least as prone to chauvinism as to universalism. Moreover, some public opinions have no way of expressing themselves and therefore of joining in the chorus of world opinion. The latter remains far less potent than the separate governments, in the world as it is. None of this means that the battles of values and philosophies must be ,resolved by struggles among states, that international violence is a *Weltgericht* of values, that there can be no compromises or no "peaceful coexistence" of moral opposites — or that when states fight it is necessarily as carriers of value systems. But it means, once again, that we shall often be very close to the pole of enmity.

The third reason for the limits on moral choice is

political. The structural and the philosophical arguments say that it is difficult for statesmen to exert moral choice because of the certainty and the pressures of competition, the power contest and the value contest. The political argument states that fair moral choice by statesmen is also made more difficult by two kinds of political handicaps. The first one is political uncertainty—the difficulty of assessing the situation. Far more than domestic statecraft, international statecraft is statecraft in the dark. It is often blind statecraft. The stateman's ethics cannot ever be a perfect ethics of responsibility, because he does not control what goes on outside, and because he normally does not even understand clearly what goes on outside. What has been happening between us and the Russians after their invasion of Afghanistan is the clearest example of this, even though we have had thirty-five years of experience, of dialog with the other side. The difficulty of assessment is created by the fact that events are always ambiguous. When you must make your decision, you often do not know what the event to which you react means. A splendid example is provided by the debate in England in 1906–1907 as to whether imperial Germany was mounting a worldwide offensive—which Britain had to stop—or was merely a clumsy, prestige-conscious nation, which the mighty British should try to accommodate. There was a comparable debate in the thirties, on whether Hitler was Hitler, or merely an impolite version of Bismarck. One key question divided the French in 1940: Was the victory of the Germans final or not? A great deal of public behavior depended on what one thought the answer was. Was Vietnam a civil war, was it an outside aggression? Are the Soviets in Afghanistan because they are afraid, or because they are cocky? And so on. The difficulty of understanding what events mean is compounded by the difficulty of assessing the effects of one's own course. We choose a policy on the basis of our (unscientific) interpretation of an event, a trend, another nation's behavior, but often ignore the fact that our own move, which we see as a mere reaction, may have unfortunate effects. We select a course, but do we know how far it will take us? When Carter seemed to drag his feet on SALT II and hasten his pace of rapprochement with China, did he calculate the effect on the Soviets? When Pétain decided for the armistice, did he know that it would lead to rather abject collaborationism a little later? Or when one rejects a course, does one know at the time whether one was wise to reject it or not? Think of the decision made by the United States to drop the atomic bomb on Japan rather than to "demonstrate" the bomb on some empty island.

The second kind of political handicap is not uncertainty, but foreclosure. The first necessity for a statesman is to preserve his political base, to maintain domestic support for his policies. But the constraints of internal moods and pressures often restrict severely his range of action abroad. Certain moral courses may be barred by domestic prohibitions; far less ethical ones may be dictated by internal imperatives. Moreover, moral choice is also hampered by the fact that different statesmen operate according to very different codes, even within the same country or the same political regime. A statesman's code is the product of his character, of his own experiences, of his upbringing, of the mood of the moment. He rarely performs according to a model of perfect rationality, weighing all options; his code tends to shut out certain alternatives, to make him blind to certain realities and deaf to certain demands, to overvalue the benefits of the preferred course and to exaggerate the costs of the discarded alternatives. Men like Chamberlain and Daladier put very high on their list of priorities the economy of lives, after the blood bath of the first World War; but, in Churchill's famous words, they got both dishonor and war. Thus moral action is impaired both by the rails on which statesmen move, which traverse only a part of the landscape, and by the fog through which the train advances.

What are the consequences of these limits on moral choice? The most evident could be called the moral inferiority of international politics. This is a domain in which, much more than in domestic politics, one pays a penalty for behaving decently. One always risks being duped; for instance if you wait angelically until your neighbor attacks you first. If one behaves too well toward outsiders—refugees, trade competitors, needy states— one may also expose oneself to a domestic backlash. Also, there is always a greater opportunity to rely on immoral methods; this was the immortal statement of Cavour: If statesmen had behaved in their private life the way they did in order to bring about the unification of Italy—lying, spying, and killing—their mothers would not have approved.

We can look at the social order as a pyramid of moralities. There is, at the bottom, the morality of the individual—let us say traditional Christian morality or its "lay," post-Enlightenment, Kantian variety. Then, there are various group moralities within the state—less capable of altruism, and prone to distinguish sharply between what is due to those who are in and what is left for those who are out. Finally there is the statesman. Machiavelli's whole work is based on the contrast between ordinary Christian ethics and the ethics of statescraft, which entails doing whatever is necessary for the good of the country—not an "immoral" code of behavior, except by Christian standards, but a different code of morality, which wills the means to the noble end of civic survival. Raison d'Etat is not an abdication from morality, but the proper morality of statecraft.

Now, in well-ordered polities, group morality—

from the family to the big pressure group—is under a double control: that of individual morality, which presumably will prevent the in/out distinction from becoming murderous, and that of the state, eager to prevent group selfishness from destroying the social order (Mafia morality is a perfect example of what happens when the double check falters). And the whole effort of Western political philosophy and Western liberalism has consisted in replacing the ethics of Machiavelli's Prince with a quasi-Christian version of statecraft morality: the ethical politics of social contract theory *á la* Locke, Rousseau, and Kant. In other words, there has been a partly successful attempt at making statecraft, concerned with the good of the national group, compatible with common-morality definitions of the good. When a recent American president behaved as a dime-store version of the Prince, he was driven out of office for having violated both the law and the spirit of the system.

The drama of international politics is that there is, as of now, no generally accepted alternative to Machiavellian statecraft. The latter has not been made illegitimate. To be sure, we have, in theory, two such alternative morals: the old Christian notion of the prince who obeys the precepts of natural law, and the Kantian version of the statesmen who adopt the principles of eternal peace. But the three factors I have discussed make it impossible for statesmen to behave as if a world community, however decentralized, had already been achieved. Wilson is an exemplary figure—both because his high ideal of non-Machiavellian statecraft ended in tragedy, and because, as the defender of his nation's interests, he sometimes acted as a good Machiavellian, "for where the very safety of the country depends upon the resolution to be taken, no considerations of justice or injustice, humanity or cruelty, nor of glory or shame, should be allowed to prevail."[9] Our problem is how to reach the stage, partially achieved in some domestic systems, of a possible non-Machiavellian ethical statecraft in international affairs—a statecraft that will not define what it is its duty to protect, the good of the nation, in ways incompatible with the good of mankind. And we must also remember that whenever enmity prevails, what J. N. Figgis rightly calls Machiavelli's philosophy of emergency, siege and self-defense will accurately describe the behavior of statesmen. The possibility of their behaving accordingly is always present, at the margin or tangentially, so to speak. As long as the structural, philosophical, and political conditions that would make an alternative ethics of statecraft practicable do not exist, recommendations or exhortations (for instance about the legitimacy of interventions for good causes) ought to be treated with considerable skepticism, on moral as well as on prudential grounds; remember Pascal: *qui veut faire l'ange fait la bête.*

The drama of moral reformers of international relations is not only that the dream of a world community with non-Machiavellian statecraft remains apolitical, but also that the Machiavellian ethics have a strong appeal. For it is not a call for the jungle, it is literally "outgroup morality." It does not advocate cynical and brutal behavior *per se;* it tends to divide mankind into those who are on our side, and our foes; it appeals to the idealism of commitment, of rewards to friends, as well as to the machismo of might, and to the competitive instinct that feeds the concern with credibility. Were it entirely the opposite of Christian, or democratic, statecraft, its appeals would be less broad. They derive both from what could be called a self-righteous perversion of such statecraft, and from the latent dissatisfaction with its meekness, with its all-too-reasonable, too uncombative character. In other words, it appeals both to the selfish instincts suppressed by Christian morality and to the fascist ones latent in many of us.

Another consequence of the limits of moral

choice consists of the dangers which exist in the field, and about which many Americans have written so eloquently that they sometimes threw out the moral baby with the murky bath. One of the dangers, already mentioned, is excessive moralizing in the abstract. This is the old critique of idealism, which wants the statesman to come straight out of the Ten Commandments, and forgets that he is bound to the here-and-now. He has to choose most of the time not between moral action and immoral action, but between competing half-moral, half-immoral, or amoral alternatives, or between a course that will strike him as moral, given his code (say, help to a "friendly" dictator in trouble) but will be denounced by people with different priorities, and a course such people would prefer but that would appear immoral to him (if it risks helping radicals hostile to the United States, in the example given). When one acts one does not choose between immorality and morality; first of all, many decisions are purely technical and have no clear moral implications; secondly, one normally has to choose between one's own brand of dubious morality and another actor's. Vietnam made all this very clear. Our trying to impose our will on the Vietcong and on Hanoi brought dreadful results; but the alternative (which we failed to prevent, and could not have prevented at a reasonable cost) was the imposition of Hanoi's will. Was it better for us to try keeping our commitment, would it have been better to spare the Vietnamese people the horrors of our war?

The other peril, which is sometimes much more serious, lies not in abstract moralizing but in self-righteousness. It is not the danger of inefficient idealism; it is the danger of effective hypocrisy. It takes two forms. One is ideological thinking, when one justifies one's discrete acts by the overall design, and looks at one's nation as the secular arm of a set of principles (whereas the abstract moralist wants to make of the statesman the humble servant of the idea, here the idea is at the mercy of the secular arm). Of course, as the French Revolution demonstrated, it is the latter that advances behind the shield of the principles. (The Soviet Union call wars of national liberation which it supports "just wars"; and the Brezhnev doctrine promises "friendly" intervention for Communist regimes in trouble.) The other form moralizing self-righteousness takes is the notion, so prominent in American writings thirty years ago, that the national interest is ethical by itself, that the defense of the interests of the state is automatically moral—which provides one with the ritualistic justification of absolutely anything, but begs the question of the compatibility of the various national interests. Both forms risk exacerbating conflict, adding violence to hypocrisy. What started as an ethical parade ends as a glorification of power—for without power the principles, or the "moral" national interest, have no chance of prevailing. The result is, at best, the tyranny of benevolence—expansion justified by "world responsibility" or "world revolution"—at worst imperialism pure and simple.

Within these limits, however, what can we do?

THE ETHICS OF FOREIGN POLICY BEHAVIOR

I began by rejecting the position of the unpolitical moralist, who believes that ethical judgments can be made in the abstract. All ethical judgments in politics, but particularly in this field, are historical judgments. They are, as the jargon would put it these days, contextual or situational; they are not separable from the concrete circumstances, from the actual cases. And I also reject the position which Kant called that of the political moralist, the person who wants to concoct a system of morals for the convenience of the statesman—in other words, the adviser of the prince who whispers in the prince's ear the principles which will justify the prince's acts. This is not what I am concerned with; I have enough colleagues who have professionally been doing this, with results which are the best evidence ever given for the merits of ivory towers. The question I want to raise is the good old Kantian question: Can one, in this field, be what he called a moral politician—whom he defined as "a man who employs the principles of political prudence in such a way that they can co-exist with morals."[10] Now this is of course a normative problem, it is a problem of *oughts,* and I know that one cannot mechanically derive an *ought* from an *is.* But one of the key necessities in this field is to avoid too big a gap between what is and what ought to be. In any system of law, or in any system of morals, there is always a gap between the *is* and the *ought,* between the empirical pattern and the norm. The gap is necessary and inevitable. If there were no gap, people would not feel any sense of obligation, or any remorse when they violate a norm. But when the gap becomes too big, the system of law or the system of morals is really doomed— to have no impact whatsoever or to be destroyed.

A skeletal outline of what ethical action in foreign policy should be like within the limits previously stated will start with some *is*es, go to some *ought*s, and end by dealing with a few objections and difficulties. Let us start with the *is.* The ethics of a statesman is and must be what Weber called an "ethics of responsibility"; it cannot be just an ethic of conviction or intentions, for all kinds of reasons. Conviction is necessary, but costs must be assessed. Intentions are normally mixed; particularly when decisions are made by groups, as they are made in most modern states. An ethics of intentions risks being one of extraordinary self-righteousness, and of the kind of callousness Weber so strongly criticized. Any moral statecraft has to be an ethics of consequences, in the sense of being concerned for the foreseeable effects. This does not mean that "whatever works is good" (whatever that means, for a key question is: For whom does it work? For the national community, at terrible costs for all others? For others, but at the expense of one's own nation's interests?). It means that the good, in politics, is not separable from its realization. The criteria of moral politics are double: sound principles, and effectiveness. A morally bad design—say, naked aggression—does not become good because it succeeds. But a morally fine one—say, a rescue operation for the freeing of hostages—does not meet the conditions of the moral politician if the details are such that success is most unlikely, or that the costs of success would be prohibitive. Politics is an art of performance; a politician with excellent intentions but incoherent or unsteady execution is not a moral politician—especially not if one effect of his clumsiness is to help far less well intentioned politicians, or politicians whose moral code is far more of the Machiavellian variety, prevail in his stead. Even a prophet-statesman, a revolutionary statesman, a Khomeini or a Lenin, and even a statesman-saint like Gandhi has to be concerned with consequences both because he is responsible to his own people and because of the bad results a neglect of consequences might have for his creed.

However, to say that he must have an ethics of responsibility does not tell you at all *how* the statesman will calculate the consequences. It depends entirely on the nature of his ends and on his view of his constituency. Concerning the latter: does he see himself as responsible above all to his people or to a more abstract conception of the nation (remember de Gaulle's distinction between France and the French) or to a larger community (the world proletariat, Islam, or, in Gandhi's case, the souls of his opponents as well as those of his supporters)? Does he see himself as responsible above all to those currently living, or to future generations whose welfare or glory he is attempting to ensure? Concerning the ends, if he is a revolutionary statesman, he will define the consequences by comparing the future he wants to reach with the bad present he wants to leave behind; and since he is likely to want to leave it behind by destroying it, he will be much more willing to use force, to use evil means, or perhaps, as in the case of Khomeini, to court martydom for his people, than if he were just your ordinary *ad hoc* pragmatic statesman campaigning in New Hampshire. If he is a statesman saint, *á la* Gandhi, he will be calculating consequences in terms of the effects of the means on the purity of the ends, because his end will be radical moral change, even if the choice of means adapted to this goal slows down liberation or social transformation.

In other words, having said that the ethics of the statesman must be an ethics of consequences, we leave the normative problem pretty much intact. And here we must leap from what must be to what ought to be. The ethics of the statesman ought to be a blend of three different elements: ends, means, and self-restraint. First of all, it has to be a morality of ends because ends are of course susceptible to moral judgment; but moral judgments of ends are never simple. At first sight, doesn't it seem obvious that certain kinds of ends are purely evil—not only according to common morality but even in a Machiavellian ethics, since they go far beyond what public safety requires: what might be called Hitlerian goals such as racial domination, the extermination and subjugation of inferior peoples, the exploitation of conquered countries, etc.? And doesn't it seem equally obvious that a goal such as national survival is necessarily good? Soon, however, the simplicity dissolves. On the one hand, who judges the morality of the ends? What we now deem repugnant was deemed moral by a huge fraction of the German people; what we see as rightful—the survival of Israel—is judged plain wrong by many Arabs. I will indicate below how to deal with that issue—the diversity of points of view, or the relativity of moral judgments; let us just remember that it is troublesome. On the other hand, in daily politics, ends are not easy to identify. Policies defined through a collective process do not always have clear ends. Also, a statesman with very evil ends can do a masterful job of disguising them for a long time. Hitler succeeded in fooling almost everybody (except people who had read *Mein Kampf*, not a best-seller) because he moved toward his horrid grandiose ends by installments—slice by slice, with means that at first seemed limited. And even ends which look rightful on the surface, like survival, dissolve once one analyzes them. For instance, do we talk about the survival of Uganda, or the survival of Idi Amin? Do we talk of the survival of an abstract entity, let us say a Pakistan which still included East Bengal, or the Federation of Nigeria, or the survival of a concrete people that may want to secede—Bangladesh, Biafra? Bad ends can be disguised, and ends which look good may be a little bit more complicated. All too often, we find ourselves in the typical Weberian situation—a conflict between equally moral ends, for instance in civil wars involving an attempted secession, or in wars that pit against each other equally legitimate but incompatible claims, as in the Arab-Israeli dispute.

In addition to a moral test, ends ought to be submitted to two others, first of all to a test of reality. A good end which has not the slightest chance of being realized—which is exactly what characterized American policy in China in the 40's, when we sought a democratic, united China under Chiang, and in Vietnam for many years, when we sought an independent, self-sustaining South Vietnam—is not good policy. And there ought to be a test of priority. If an end is good, it does not mean necessarily that it should be put on top. There are, inevitably, competing objectives that may be more pressing, and morally more important. I will attempt a more precise definition of moral ends in the next chapters, dealing with major issues in foreign policy. But precisely because the simple examination of ends is not enough, we must move from the ends to the means. A valid end does not meet the demands of moral politics if it requires a price that is excessive for oneself or for others: Pétain tried to obtain France's survival by concessions that mortgaged both French honor and French independence, just as at Munich Chamberlain and Daladier tried to save peace (and to give themselves more time for rearmament) by sacrificing Czechoslovakia. Nor is a valid end morally acceptable if it requires means more evil than the evil to be avoided or redressed. For instance, the Palestinians' original end was to redress the injustice committed against them by throwing the Israelis into the sea. A valid end can be undermined by the wrong choice of means. The goal of Israeli security is certainly a good one, but not if it has to be achieved by creating massive insecurity for the Arabs, and particularly for the Palestininians. Justice for the Palestinians is a rightful end, but not if it entails indiscriminate terror against innocent Israelis (or a presumption of collective guilt that eliminates all distinctions). In other words, international relations is an endless chain of ends and means. Today's means shape tomorrow's ends. The choice of means is particularly important either when the range of choice of ends is narrow—when the ends are almost dictated by the international situation, that is, in periods of extcme enmity, or on the contrary, when the range of choice of ends is quite broad, when the statesman can choose among ends which are all morally fairly plausible or all morally mixed (as

had been the case for us in Vietnam). It is morally necessary to choose means which are not destructive of one's
end through coercion or corruption; secondly, the means
must be proportional both to the end, and to the importance of the end in the hierarchy of one's goals; and
finally, one ought to choose means which do not entail
costs of values greater than the cost of not using these
means.

One must nevertheless recognize that the calculation of effects, in international affairs, is always hazardous. Because of the huge political handicap of uncertainty, a statesman can never be sure that his means will
deliver the results he expects. Therefore, even an ethics
of consequences needs to be saved from the perils of
unpredictability and from the temptations of Machiavellianism by a corset of firm principles guiding the choice
of ends and of means—by a dose of ethics of conviction
covering both goals and instruments. What this entails is
indicated by the final ingredient: a morality of self-
restraint. The purpose of moral action in international
affairs ought to be to diminish the strain of the antinomies that weigh on the statesmen and on the citizens. We
are all torn between our duties as citizens and our vaguer
duties as members of mankind. A morality of self-
restraint entails simply taking into account the existence
of the moral claims of others.

This in turn has a number of consequences. The
first is the need to observe the principle of self-
determination. It can be abused. There is no "objective"
way of defining a nation—since the borders of many
states are purely artificial, the principle of self-
determination may be deeply subversive of the existing
order; and when it is claimed by tribes, minorities, ethnic
groups within existing nations, it seems like a recipe for
chaos, in full contradiction of the trends of economic
interdependence. (Every unhappy group does not have a

right to establish its own nation. Many nations are successful blends of different ethnic or cultural entities; a state that is not yet a nation deserves a chance to create one.) However, the possible excesses—some of which result from claims provoked or exacerbated by the mismanagement and brutalities of domestic systems—are no reason for refusing to acknowledge the validity of the principle itself, or for subordinating its application to a higher but ill-defined ideal of justice. Justice itself requires that the right be granted; for there is no more certain injustice than alien rule imposed against the will of a people.[11] Self-determination is a precondition for peaceful coexistence. And if one ever wants to go beyond the nation-state, recognizing the right of people to their own nation is the first step; you cannot go beyond by avoiding it.

A second consequence is the immorality of any policy of universal domination, because it can only be imposed by force. And the last one is the immorality of any national policy of universal or very large-scale intervention (which does not mean, we shall see it later, that some interventions are not allowable). To be sure, foreign policy, especially that of great powers, cannot refrain from intervening abroad—refusing to intervene (against a tyrannical government, or by giving aid to a needy people) is itself a form of intervention. But I am referring to the more extreme forms, military or not, aimed not merely at influence but at control. They are incompatible with the right of a nation to determine its own destiny. A fuller discussion will be provided in the next chapter.

One might object that a morality of self-restraint simply perpetuates the traditional game of international politics with all its antinomies. But one must remember that the first duty of the statesman is to his own community; he is not at the helm in order to abolish the race, although it is proper to ask him to make it more moderate and sportslike. A policy that aims at protecting the nation's interest while minimizing the risks for all others is morally preferable to a more ambitious attempt at transcending the game, which weakens the international order and leaves all nations less secure. One may also object that by equating existing regimes with the underlying (and often oppressed) nations, self-restraint actually allows the former to commit a host of injustices and to make the people a victim of their state. However, self-restraint does not mean endorsing the status quo. A diplomacy of self-restraint may be used to make the world a better place, and while it rules out attempts at extreme manipulation or imperialism, it does not rule out, as the next chapters will show, attempts at fighting a variety of injustices abroad. To show regard for the rights of others means both refraining from trampling them and helping others to rescue these rights when they are trampled or ignored.

Indeed, the ethics of the statesman ought to be guided by the imperative of moving the international arena from the state of a jungle to that of a society, because the moral opportunities available to all of us—not only to the statesman—depend on the state of the international system. Moral opportunities, in every milieu, depend on the social framework. If (as in primitive societies) integration is total, there is no moral choice at all. This is not a danger that threatens international relations. If the social framework disintegrates, there are no longer sufficient opportunities for moral choice. In international affairs they are, as we have seen, limited and pervertible—but not always to the same extent. The closer the international system is to a jungle, the closer we are to the floor of survival, the less opportunity for choice we have, the more values we have to sacrifice, the more plausible the statesman's claim of necessity becomes, the more we will be tempted to accept the "morality of struggle"—and either resign ourselves to endless competition, or put a moral dressing on it, in either case restricting our duties to our own community and, at most, to its supporters or clients. On the contrary, the more moderate the system is, the greater the range of moral choice for all of us, the greater the possibility for the statesman to look at the world in terms other than us vs. them—to try to move from what I called a Machiavellian morality of public safety to a more universal morality that accepts the rightful claims of others; so that the question: right or good for whom? is no longer answered: exclusively for the statesman's community.

In a sense we have gone back to Kant in two ways. First of all, he was not wrong to believe that if one wants to move in that direction, one prerequisite is domestic: what he called constitutional government. Not necessarily because the people are always for peace, whereas autocrats are for war. We have seen imperialistic and bellicose democracies. But domestically repressive governments often promote immoderate statecraft outside and need outside successes to maintain their grip inside. It is much more likely that moral judgments on ends and means will be observed if there is a certain amount of popular control over what the government does. All of the precepts I advocated suppose a great deal of public discussion, a very limited amount of secrecy, a very limited possibility of cooking up Machiavellian schemes in the dark. A morality of self-restraint is compatible with liberal nationalism. It is incompatible with the kind of nationalism that developed in many nations by the end of the nineteenth century, but was at its most acute in countries which had no constitutional or representative governments.

Secondly, the guidelines I have listed can exploit the two "oughts" which I think emerge from the present

international situation. All states want to survive in a
nuclear world, and all states, or almost all, need each
other for their own economic and social development. It
was Kant who predicted that nations would move toward
peace not because of the moral will and virtue of human
beings, but because of the terror of modern weapons,
and because of greed—people being dragged to the good
by the horror of modern war and by material need.
Those two concerns—survival and interdependence—
are the only tenuous, uneven, contentious common
threads.

This sketchy discussion raises two categories of
questions or objections. I have been talking about rules of
behavior. The first question is: Rules for whom? There is
a horizontal aspect to the question, and there is a vertical
one. The horizontal one is the old dilemma of relativism;
the values and directions I have suggested are not accepted by everybody. I have pointed out that conflicts of
ethical codes characterize international affairs. The solution to this is certainly not to accept relativism and give in.
For giving in simply means refusing to judge, and that
means not merely accepting the validity of all codes, but
in effect yielding to the strongest, neither of which is
acceptable. One has to recognize the diversity of values,
and the close connection between them and a society's
social structure and culture—another reason for self-
restraint and prudence in acting abroad. But then one
must go on and make one's own decision—a step both
necessary and arbitrary. It is necessary to protect and
promote one's own values if one believes in them, especially when one deems some other codes to be destructive
of all values; and it is arbitrary, because no system of
values can claim to be the only good and true one; but so
be it. One must not confuse tolerance for diversity, and
for those values of other people that are merely different
from ours, with the acceptance of practices and policies

that violate our notion of humanity. To do the latter would mean abandoning "the element of universalization which is present in any morality."[12] If the values we try to promote are values which make the coexistence of peoples and value systems possible, there is no need to be ashamed of it. In two cases I mentioned earlier, the Germans in the 30's and the Arab-Israeli dispute, the answer certainly is not relativism—"all claims are equally valid." The solution, quite simply, is that one had to resist the Nazis, whose code required the destruction of "inferior" races and value systems, but without exterminating the German people; and that should have had some consequences on how one ought to have waged the war. And one ought to recognize Israel's existence and security needs, but not at the expense of justice for the claims of the other side.

The vertical dimension of the question of "rules for whom" is the problem of cosmopolitanism. Are the rules of moral conduct I have been trying to suggest rules of behavior among governments, which define rights and duties of states such as the respect of treaties, or the equality of states, or the principle of collective security? Or are they also rules of behavior for the benefit of the citizens of other states? If you want to rephrase the question, do states have rights because they are states, independently of what happens inside them? Or if you prefer to rephrase it in a different way, already mentioned above, Justice for whom? Are we trying simply to define rules of justice for the states, or for the people? This is a very controversial question; it opposes, as one author puts it, the traditional international law conception of the morality of states, "states, not persons, (as) the subjects of international morality,"[13] versus what could be called "cosmopolitan morality," in which the only real beneficiaries of rights and holders of duties are persons. My answer would be that it has to be a mix of both. There is justification for the morality of states. States have rights and duties as the main actors in world affairs. The relation between the rights of a state and the degree to which the state or the regime is based on the implicit consent of the persons that live under its jurisdiction will be explored later. But insofar as each national group is deemed to have the right to organize its own state and to exert autonomy through it, the state benefits from the presumption that it is the expression of the national wish to independence. We have a right to be French and not Germans, to be Americans and not Soviets, to be Afghans and not a mere republic incorporated in big brother's domain. This is the foundation of the state's rights and duties. The Pol Pot regime was quite illegitimate at home—it is the least one could say—but still Cambodians are entitled to form the state of Cambodia, and not a province of Vietnam.

On the other hand, it is clear that there is a relation between the rights of individuals and the rights of states. The latter are not unlimited and unconditional. States are artificial constructs. Also, statesmen affect by their behavior the lives of people abroad; and even though there is not yet any community of mankind, we in many nations that are not closed off begin to be affected by germs of cosmopolitan consciousness. Many of us are becoming a little more than pure nationals to whom other men, being foreigners, are nothing. In other words, we are in a period of transition, in which there are twin dangers. One is to neglect the cosmopolitan germs—and therefore to treat states as if they were indeed totally sovereign or absolutes. But the other danger is to destroy those germs of cosmopolitanism either by advocating sweeping cosmopolitan measures while forgetting that their enforcement depends on the existing states—a sure way to insure their evaporation or distortion; or by removing too soon the protection which statehood provides to citizens against domination by foreigners. For the real choice for most of us is not between being, say, Americans and being citizens of the world; it is a choice between being Americans and being somebody else's satellites or victims.

The second set of questions is not rules for whom, but what kinds of rules. This has a general and a specific focus. The general question could be phrased, "interest versus morality." If the statesman is bound to the interests of his state, if he must be selfish for the state's survival, security, and interests, can one really talk about morality at all? Is not the best one can hope for a kind of relaxed Hobbesianism? One should not exaggerate. Selfishness and total disregard of moral restraints are not synonymous. Even Weber wrote that he admired the statesman who, having reached a certain point, says: here I stand, I can do no other. It is true that state altruism is not very frequent, nor can it always be commended because, after all, the statesman's duty is to look after the interests of his people. However, all statesmen have a tendency to justify their acts in moral terms and not in those of Machiavellian morality, but according to standards other than Raison d'Etat; even in Thucydides, when statesmen, in their speeches, argue about their respective positions and ambitions, they reason in moral terms of rights and wrongs. This is more than a tribute of vice to virtue. It is an acknowledgment of the fact that statesmen find a need to go beyond mere Hobbesian behavior. Moreover, the ways in which statesmen defend their nations' interests vary a great deal. They very often include moral considerations in defining the national interest, by adding milieu to possession goals, by making long-range considerations prevail over short-term gains. Also, it is quite possible to show the bad impact of either recurrent immoral behavior or of shockingly evil conduct on one's interest. It was not good for the interests of France and

Britain to have behaved at Munich the way they did. Nor did Hitler's methods found a thousand-year Reich. Only if one took the position that the sole genuine morality is that which requires selfless behavior, would the gap between interest and ethical action be unbridgeable. But "it is quite unrealistic to force onto...anyone...an exclusive disjunction between the prudential and the moral," precisely because these two categories "leave out, in fact, almost everything" about human motivations.[14] The conflict between interest and morality should not be dramatized, and the task of moral politics is to bring the two together.

The more specific question is: what criteria of moral judgment are appropriate for international politics? There is a debate between utilitarians and champions of Kantian morality or, if you prefer, an ethics of rights and duties, "Thou shalt do this" or "Thou shalt not do that"—categorical imperatives. Utilitarians have a *prima facie* strong case. They can argue as follows: If the sad necessity of international relations is that one must make morality and interest coincide, and also that one must always weigh the consequences of what one does, would not then the ethics of international relations be necessarily utilitarian? Should not the statesman aim at the greatest good for the greatest number, at the greatest happiness, or the long-term utility as decided by rational people? Is it not more fitting than the morality of absolutes, of the categorical imperative, or the Decalog?

This is not necessarily true, even though happiness and utility are obviously worthy goals. To say that the statesman must calculate consequences, that is, worry about how his precepts will be realized, does not mean that the precept must be the calculus of happiness. Why should it not be a calculus of the best way of promoting a fundamental right or of ensuring a categorical prohibition? Only if it could be shown that such rights or prohibitions cannot be enforced except at disastrous cost would the utilitarian preference make sense. Utilitarianism is *an* ethics of consequences; that does not make it *the* ethics of international affairs. Moreover, the criteria on which it relies are quite problematic. In a sense, they beg the key question of foreign policy behavior: whose (greatest) good is the statesman enhancing? In a pure "state of war," there is no general standard of utility—see Rousseau again: it is only the happiness of his own "pseudo-species" that the statesman can worry about; for in situations of total enmity, what is useful to me cannot be useful to my enemy. If the competition relaxes, there is still a danger of *my* trying to impose my notions of happiness and utility on *you*—and as Kant has shown they are far more subjective than considerations of basic rights and wrongs. Statecraft, quite properly, often gives priority to other concerns: one can argue that only when basic issues of legitimacy, authority, and freedom are settled is the road to a politics of happiness or welfare open. Moreover, different kinds of utility or disutility are nonfungible, and policy decisions must take into account many nonquantifiable, noncomparable elements; the effects of different kinds of decisions on happiness and utility are equally hard to assess and to compare. In other words, there is no substitute for a weighing of alternatives, and utilitarianism, far from providing easy guidelines or shortcuts, tends to become excessively rubbery, to split into infinite varieties, and to breed an exuberant casuistry in its attempt to encompass an unmanageable reality. It ends up often as a vast exercise in ex post rationalization, and it is open to the criticism that in its emphasis on "simple-seeming . . . calculation," "it often appears to imply that" dubious acts, "apart from their resultant harm and benefits, are in themselves neutral."[15]

In international affairs concerns of order and status, honor and trust, safety and ideology are either prior to considerations of pleasure and pain, or impossible to translate into calculations of happiness and utility. Here such calculations are especially uncertain; we are in the domain of uncertainty. Utilitarianism is better at giving one a good conscience than at providing a compass. The answer to the question must therefore be one which is very unsatisfactory for philosophers (but as I said earlier I am not one of them). The morality of international relations will simply have to be a mix of commands and of utilitarian calculations. The commands cannot be followed at any cost; "Thou shalt not kill" or "Thou shalt not lie" can never be pushed so far that the cost clearly becomes a massive disutility to the national interest (how much of a disutility is bearable depends on alternatives, on the statesman's conception of the national interest, and on the nature of the system). On the other hand, purely utilitarian ethics simply cannot cope with the complexity and the shortcomings of the calculations statesmen must make; the advantage of imperatives is that they provide at least a sense of direction.

~~ 2 ~~

The Use of Force

TAMING THE UNTAMABLE

*T*HE PROBLEM of the use of force is central to the subject of ethics and foreign policy. In the first place, the use of force in international affairs is obviously the greatest obstacle to moral behavior; the belief so well expressed by General Sherman that "war is hell," and that therefore there is nothing one should or can do to "refine" it, is a manifestation of this. As long as states use force against one another, citizens will be torn between their duties as citizens and their consciousness as reasonable and moral beings whose thoughts and feelings transcend borders. Also, wars provide the greatest opportunities for national self-righteousness and for the denial of the humanity and the rights of others. Finally, it is in war that the greatest opportunity exists for statesmen, and for military commanders, to plead necessity, to argue that they really have no choice, that what they do is literally imposed upon them by military imperatives. And yet the use of force remains the essence of the international milieu despite all of the efforts of lawyers and statesmen to do away with it, despite the League of Nations and the Briand-Kellogg pact and despite the U.N. Charter.

The contradiction between attempts at moralizing international politics and the actors' free resort to force accounts for the ideological and historical diversity

of the ways of dealing with this subject. Ideologically, at
any given moment we find a range of attitudes which go
at one end from absolute pacifists, adepts of non-violence
who reject any use of force at all, to the glorification of
war at the other end—as a historical necessity and a moral
good, as a force which, as Hegel saw it, makes people
transcend the selfishness, mediocrity, and inevitable corruption of civil society and tests the virtue of citizens and
states. Historically, the attempts at introducing ethical
considerations into this subject have gone through three
very different phases. Many centuries were dominated
by the "just war" theory, which was a doctrine of restraints
on the causes and on the conduct of war before the
sovereign territorial state became the prevalent structure
of the international system. Then, during a second
phase, which lasted two and a half or three centuries, the
age of sovereignty, war was treated essentially as a morally neutral fact and therefore could be indulged in by
states whenever they had a reason for it; the only rules
which tried to deal with war were rules on how to fight,
but not on why to fight: rules on the conduct of war.
Finally, for the last half century or so, an extraordinary
discrepancy has grown between the collapse, for ideological and technological reasons, of all the restraints which
had been more or less carefully worked out in the past,
and the frantic search for new, more drastic restraints on
the other. So that the literature which now deals with the
problem of ethics and the use of force can be seen as an
attempt at building up a new "just war" theory, for an age
in which the territorial sovereign state is still very much
with us—indeed, it keeps proliferating—but war has
gone completely out of hand and threatens to destroy
sovereignty itself.

        This literature has been growing rapidly in the
recent past. One most important addition is Michael
Walzer's *Just and Unjust Wars*. Since I share his moral

theory and agree with many of his precepts, much of this chapter will read like a gloss on his work. I will again begin with a look at the dilemmas and then suggest some answers.

It is useful to start with an examination of the old "just war" theory which remains the only coherent doctrine that has ever lasted on this subject for no less than a dozen centuries.[1] Looking at what would happen to it if it were applied in the twentieth century tells us a great deal about the ethical dilemmas in the realm of force.[2] The most obvious point is the inadequacy of traditional "just war" theory to the world in which we are, and the roots of the trouble are fairly clear. There is an old root and there is a new one. The old one dates from the beginning of the age of the territorial state. In a fragmented world of territorial states without a sovereign over them, in a world in which each actor resorts to self-preservation and self-help, how can one assure that moral imperatives dealing with force will be neither so loose as to permit practically everything in the competition of states, or so strict as to be absolutely inapplicable given that competition? The new root of trouble which has been added by the twentieth century is also very obvious—how can any system of restraints be respected in the new technological circumstances of this age? In other words, even if one could overcome the fundamental contradiction between restraints and sovereign states, which is not very easy, could one still corset war, given the technology which is now in use? "Technology cannot make men bad, but it may surely give rise to circumstances in which it is increasingly difficult to be good."[3]

The old doctrine was an attempt at dealing with the problem of force not by a ban but by a harness. The Catholic writers from Saint Augustine on realized that violence was part of human life and could not be suppressed or denied in the earthly city; the problem became one of using it for the good of people rather than for evil. The result of this attempt at harnessing force was a series of restraints both on ends and on means. War would be just only if fought with the right intention by the prince—peace and justice, not revenge—and waged for a just cause which could be either self defense *or* a cause of sufficient concern to the community of mankind—redressing a serious injury to one's people or one's possessions. As for the means, they were to be restricted by a series of objective and subjective restraints. The objective restrictions were quite numerous—one was allowed to use only means which had a reasonable chance of success, only means which were proportional to the stakes, and there was the most important objective prescription of noncombatant immunity. As for the subjective restraints, the most famous is the formidable double effect rule, which said that an act of war that was likely to have an evil effect, such as killing noncombatants, would be morally tolerable only under two conditions: first of all, that the direct intended effect be morally acceptable (and of course, given the rule of proportionality, superior to the evil effect) and second, that the evil effects be unintended, and not a means toward the end. The whole theory was a remarkable blend of different elements; it took the two perfectly contradictory Christian impulses, one toward pacifism and the other toward crusades, and partly blended them, partly restrained them both. It was a mix of formal rules, like noncombatant immunity, and utilitarian precepts, like the calculation of consequences; it was both an ethics of intentions and an ethics of actions.

The reason it cannot be followed purely and simply and expected to work in the contemporary world is that it was based on assumptions derived from a totally different political and technological universe—and also because it encounters all the difficulties of utilitarianism. If one took those criteria seriously today, their application could produce one of two things, which happen to be exactly opposite, and both bad. If one applied them in one way, one could easily get disaster by excessive permissiveness. Take the notion that a just war can be a war for self-defense. If it is left as vague as this, it could easily lead to generalization of preventive or preemptive war (should one argue that under modern technological conditions, survival requires one to strike before one is attacked), and in fact to a generalization of war altogether, because it does not tell you against what self-defense is just—against an armed attack? A seizure of hostages? An expropriation of enterprises? The mistreatment of one's nationals? For instance, under the old doctrine could not the British and French have validly argued, as they did in 1956, that Nasser's closing of the Suez Canal, which was not done by force, justified a reply by force; and could not the United States have argued, as it did with a great deal of tortuous skill, that the placing of Soviet missiles in Cuba, which were pointed but not shot at the United States, would have justified a reply by force, an attack on those bases? Similarly, the notion that a nondefensive war can be just if it is fought for a cause that is objectively serious enough to be of general concern could be an extraordinary source of conflict generalization. Both the Brezhnev doctrine and what was sometimes called a Johnson doctrine about our right to save from communism countries such as the Dominican Republic could be used with reference to the old theory.

On the other hand, if one applied it in a more strict and rigorous way, the conclusion would be that all modern large-scale war is unjust. Take the fairly careful blend of ends and means which the old doctrine entails; even good ends, like a valid cause or self-defense, if fought with the modern means, stop being attempts at vindicating the social order. In just war doctrine the ends to which just wars are fought amount to a protection, through the use of force, of the international social order which has been violated by an attack on certain fundamental rights; but with the modern means of war the pursuit of even good ends can become a factor of destruction of the whole fabric of mankind.

The doctrine was elaborated for three sets of circumstances which are no longer with us; first of all, for a world in which the Princes were sufficiently Christian to have the "right intention" required, or in which the Church was sufficiently strong in authority and power to define and interpret morality—not for a world in which the right intention becomes a matter of self-righteous and self-serving self-interpretation.

Secondly, it was elaborated for wars that were very different from the present Frankenstein monsters which we call total wars—whether they are "total" in the sense of all-out wars with modern technologies of destruction, or "total" because they are political wars for control of a population, fought by rival factions in a civil strife or by guerrillas. The just war doctrine states that it is fair to use means which have a chance of success; on the other hand, they must be proportional to the stakes. If one argues that it is fair to use whatever has a reasonable chance of success, sometimes the only means which have such a chance will happen to be totally disproportionate to the stakes; think of what is sometimes necessary to win an antiguerrilla war—think of Vietnam, or of the Soviets in Afghanistan. Moreover, the whole notion of proportionality of means to the stakes becomes meaningless as a restraint in modern war for a very simple reason. Both World War I and World War II produced an escalation of stakes. When people throw millions of men into the battlefield, and suffer enormous losses, and have to give themselves reasons for the horror, the stakes escalate; if you apply the principle that means are just as long as they are proportional to the stakes, once the stakes become defined as nothing less than the salvation of mankind, or the victory of a sacred cause, the proportionality of means becomes a rather sinister joke. The best example is the dropping of the atomic bomb on Japan. If one thinks that unconditional surrender and the total destruction of the forces of evil are indeed the right stakes of a just war, then abbreviating it by dropping the bomb becomes perfectly arguable. Modern wars also play havoc with the double effect rule. It says essentially that there should be no direct intentional killing of civilians; if one takes that literally, it would eliminate—which would be very good indeed—all obliteration bombing clearly aimed at the civilians; but it would still allow enormous "incidental" killings. The United States in North Vietnam did not intentionally bomb civilian targets, but the military targets it selected allowed for fairly large "incidental" massacres—unless one accepts Robert W. Tucker's distinction that these kinds of massacres, while they are not desired, are nevertheless intended, in which case one comes back to the moral outlawing of all the means of modern war.[4] But if one outlaws the means of modern war, then even a just war of self-defense could become impossible to wage in certain circumstances—the "moral" power would be at the mercy of its foe. (I am thinking of the argument sometimes made on behalf of Britain's resort to city bombing in November 1940, when such bombing was practically the only means available to Britain.) Modern war, given its technology, provokes enormous inevitable killings of civilians which may be indeed "incidental," unintended, but which are perfectly well known and accepted.

Thirdly, the doctrine was elaborated for circumstances in which there was a fairly clear distinction between peace and war; and yet we now live in an age in which peace and war have become blurred, not only because wars are seldom declared, and because especially the big powers want to fight (often through proxies)*and* keep talking, but above all because war often takes the form of powers intervening violently in the violent domestic affairs of other states without respecting the traditional rules of international law which assimilated civil war to interstate war once it had reached a certain level; and also because what dominates our lives is deterrence, an extraordinary condition in which one lives in peace while preparing for war, in which one accumulates all the means of war while saying that they are aimed at peace. Nothing is more disturbing or instructive than reading theologians, twisting, wriggling, and squirming when they face the problem of deterrence. After all, one can argue that the United States, the Soviet Union, and the other nations which accumulate the means of nuclear deterrence, have the right intention, which is to maintain peace, and a good cause, the avoidance of war. However, deterrence consists of threatening to do evil, and the effectiveness, the credibility of deterrence, depends on making oneself able to get the adversary to believe that one is indeed capable of carrying out the threat of mass murder. Even if you think that what really matters is the right intention and a good cause, you have to remember that in order to make the threat credible, in other words in order to maintain peace, since many factors make the balance of terror delicate, statesmen must escalate the arms race, and cease relying exclusively on increasingly less credible threats of instant annihilation; and even though more limited options are supposed to make war less destructive should deterrence fail, the likelihood remains that if deterrence fails these restraints might collapse, and destruction would be colossal.

Such is the plight of the just war theory; and the reactions to it by those who have tried to remain within its inspiration and intellectual orbit have been rather unsatisfactory. For instance, the pronouncements of the

Vatican II Council on the subject of war do not take us very far. The Church explicitly recognized the right of lawful self-defense if all peace efforts have failed, but it never explained what self-defense meant—against what kinds of crimes or violations it was legitimate—and it never pronounced on whether anticipatory self-defense, preemptive strikes, like the Israeli *Blitz* in 1967, were legitimate or not. Vatican II condemned genocide, total war, the arms race, and the "indiscriminate destruction" of cities and whole areas. This fudged the issues raised by the rule of double effect: what about the "discriminate" destruction of cities, what about unintended, indirect, and nevertheless perfectly effective obliteration? Not a word was said about the morality of deterrence, except for a cryptic sentence stating that "many people" deem it the most effective way of maintaining "some sort of peace" at present.

As a result, theologians have scattered all over the field; some, mainly Catholics, have retreated into nuclear pacifism, which is a simple position, but not one backed by the Council. Others, mainly Protestants, have resorted to the kind of casuistry which atheists in the past liked to call Jesuitic. Many of them have been looking for a way in which, in the world of total war, one could somehow go back to just wars by waging limited wars; that the moral problem of war could be solved, if only the qualitative factor introduced by nuclear weapons could somehow be removed. But there are two difficulties with this attempt. First, what kinds of limitations can one advocate, that are really convincing in this day and age? Should they be limitations on ends? Self-interpretation would soon breed distortions.[5] Should they be restraints on means? Let us assume that states agree to limit their armaments efforts on one front; this may encourage unlimited efforts on the others—we have seen this even in the so-called SALT process, where it has been called the sausage effect: you constrain the sausage in one or two points and it bulges everywhere else, you limit one kind of weapon, and you compensate by building huge amounts of those that are not banned, so that in between arms control agreements, the nuclear forces of the two superpowers have increased as never before. Similarly, let us suppose that the nuclear states manage to agree on something which many experts and theologians like, a statement by each one of the nuclear powers that it would not use nuclear weapons first. This sounds like a perfectly moral and fine "categorical imperative" attempt to limit war; however, one has to reintroduce the consideration of consequences. It might encourage nuclear proliferation—by those states which had felt protected by a superpower as long as that superpower was willing to threaten or hint that it might use nuclear weapons first if the ally is attacked. Another try at finding morally tolerable limits reminiscent of the old tradition is the notion, expertly upheld by Paul Ramsey, that limited counterforce nuclear war would be morally right, by contrast with large-scale countercity war, which would be the result if deterrence by threats of mutual assured destruction failed. I will return to this issue later; but clearly there are formidable obstacles. A limited, clean, surgical counterforce war requires perfect command and control, and fortunately nobody has ever had any experience of such a war. Also, this suggestion assumes that it is easy to distinguish countercity war from counterforce war; that may be possible when one buries one's missiles in desert areas, as the superpowers in part have done; but the distinction makes absolutely no sense when one thinks of Europe, where all of the military objectives, which would be the targets of counterforce warfare, happen to be situated a few kilometers from major cities because of high population density.

The attempt at "saving" the morality of limited

war encounters a second difficulty as well: what if the successful quest for limits makes war look less horrible, and makes it thereby more likely? One has to weigh, against the "attractiveness" of limited war (as opposed to nuclear holocaust), not only the possibly lesser deterrent value of the prospect, but also the chance that the "limited" war might not remain limited. This is another drawback of counterforce objectives, and of the no-first-use proposal, which might make more likely conventional wars that risk not remaining conventional if the loser, feeling trapped by necessity, resorts to his nuclear weapons after all. And even if the "limited" war stays limited, but only in the sense of not being nuclear, does anyone deem a conventional World War III moral? Those who ask: What if nuclear deterrence fails, and suggest measures to keep war limited in that case, should be asked in return: What if a repetition of World War II worked?

These are the dilemmas one faces when one tries to rescue the just war theory. However, there is no need to abdicate moral judgment yet. We must try to find some guidelines that address themselves to the moral issues of modern war, and thus go beyond either strategic engineering or legal exegesis. There are two kinds of moral issues, which shall be examined successively: those that face the statesmen, and those which the citizens must confront.

STATES AND THE MORALITY OF WAR

The problems faced by statesmen have traditionally been divided into those raised by the ends of war and those raised by the means. For what ends can a war be morally justifiable? Here the dilemma of the moralist is particularly acute. It is very easy to deride utilitarians. They would say that a war can be just if resorting to it increases the common utility or the general happiness—it is not a very satisfactory notion, because when states are engaged in intense conflict with one another, the whole notion of common utility becomes rather fatuous; each state will be easily convinced that its victory will of course maximize general happiness or utility (two very different notions) and that its failure to stand up to its foe will be a cause of general disaster. Moreover, given the uncertainty of war, accurate calculations of utility are practically impossible—the belligerents of 1914 expected a short war. Finally, even when there are reasonable utilitarian grounds, as in the case of traditional balance of power wars which states fought in order to prevent a troublemaker from getting too threatening or too large (so that states trying to restrain the troublemaker by force could argue that such wars were indeed useful, because the troublemaker would otherwise destroy the whole international social order), this argument can lead to an extraordinary generalization of wars; can one know how the troublemaker would have behaved if one had not confronted him by force first? How can one be sure that a successful war won't incite the checkmated troublemaker to find new and more destructive ways of upsetting the status quo?

On the other hand, if one believes that utilitarianism is so elastic and so vague that one has to go back to categorical imperatives, of the kind that have been included in the Charter of the United Nations for instance, notions such as self-defense, or community causes such as collective security against aggression risk producing the maximum hypocrisy and the maximum escalation of self-righteous claims in a decentralized milieu. As long as we are in a world of self-help, where each state will interpret the categorical imperative in its own way, all states ought to be under suspicion. This suspicion could be removed if there were some impartial judge, deciding which of the claims are valid; but there is no such common judge; the least one can say about the only one that exists—the United Nations—is that it is neither very effective (think of the veto-ridden Security Council) nor very impartial (think of the General Assembly). So I would maintain a presumption against any state which says "my cause is just." This doesn't dispense us from having to look at what kinds of moral rules ought to be followed. It puts us on guard against easy distortions.

A doctrine of moral limitations of the states' resort to force can be based on one of two sets of foundations.[6] It can rest on the idea of justice, as in Charles Beitz's political theory; he rejects the analogy between individuals and states and denies that the latter have a basic right to national self-preservation; he justifies interventions against unjust states, and subordinates the claim for self-determination to the need for justice. There are two problems with this approach. One is philosophical; while Beitz may be right in challenging the moral foundation of the principle of state autonomy, his failure ever to define the appropriate principles of justice leaves a gaping hole at the very heart of his theory. Moreover, it is blissfully unpolitical, since he keeps forgetting that it is the very states he distrusts that will have to carry out the principles of justice (whatever these may be), and he ignores the fact that for most persons justice is not a disembodied ideal, but one that can best be realized through an appropriate state of their own.

The alternative is what Michael Walzer calls the legalist paradigm, which assumes that "states actually possess rights more or less as individuals do"; they form an international society, and "the rights of the member states must be vindicated, for it is only by virtue of those rights that there is a society at all."[7] Does this mean that states are indeed assimulated to individuals? Actually, states derive their rights from two sources. One could be

called international society, the other and more fundamental is domestic society. International society grants
states legal rights and duties in recognition of their effective control of a territory and population—as a consequence of their existence. There is, as I have stated before, a presumption that the existence of a state derives
from the needs and consent of its people. It is a presumption which lasts as long as the people have not destroyed
it, by abolishing the state and replacing it, through secession or merger; or as long as the state has not been
destroyed by outside force. Clearly, a state established by
external force, or internally oppressive, is in a generally
dubious position; but Augustine already recognized that
"a state might act unjustly and still have legitimacy," "be a
jural commonwealth irrespective of its moral character."[8]
A state based on morally wrong foundations nevertheless
has not only legal rights but moral rights because, as
Walzer puts it, if its legal rights are not upheld, international society will collapse into a state of war or universal
tyranny. Hence, as he again argues, the validity of the
theory of aggression—the moral right, indeed the moral
duty to resist it, since it undermines the whole international society.

 Even though the rights of territorial integrity and
political sovereignty belong to the states, the extent to
which the latter do actually owe their existence to the
"special sort" of consent Walzer describes—the common
life shaped by shared experiences—affects their "moral
standing." To repeat: an unjust state—set up by a con-
queror, or denying self-determination to some of its
people—has a diminished moral stature. But the key
question is whether the rottenness of its domestic foundations justifies outside attack; whether the absence of
legitimate domestic foundations eliminates its rights as a
member of international society. We are in a dilemma: to
answer yes may breed the chaos or tyranny Walzer warns

against, by allowing each state to attack those members of international society it decrees morally unfit to exist. But to answer no seems to suggest that states are entities with rights of their own, independently of the human beings that constitute them. We will see later on that the dilemma is less acute than it seems.

If one accepts, on the whole, the legalist paradigm, which is based not on the idea that international society is a morally blameless structure, but on the notion that it is only in and through the states that (so far) individuals can assert and exert their own rights and that states therefore need to secure their independence and integrity, the most generally accepted cause for which a state can fight an ethically justified war is self-defense. The U.N. Charter's recognition of this has led to an escalation of claims of self-defense.[9] Such a claim is morally acceptable only under certain conditions. It must be a self-defense against an armed attack, or against an absolutely vital security interest, such as the other side's violation of treaty provisions designed for the protection of the now threatened power (cf. Hitler's remilitarization of the Rhineland in 1936), or what Kissinger once referred to as "economic strangulation"—a decision to withhold effectively economic resources without which the clients' economies would collapse. A war (by which I mean the actual use of military force on a large scale, not a mere declaration of war, or a declaration followed by a blockade) would not be a valid reply to a seizure of hostages (this does not mean that a blockade would be appropriate, in the case of Iran—only that the moral judgments to be brought to bear would concern means rather than ends). A claim of self-defense to justify a war on behalf of secondary interests, or against threats that can be handled effectively—if at certain cost—as many can, without resort to force, is not morally acceptable. This is why the British and the French in 1956 could not validly claim that the nationalization of the Suez Canal (unaccompanied by any explicit violation of the Constantinople Convention) was of such vital importance that only force was the proper answer; and it has become very clear ever since that it was not the nationalization of the canal which threatened their interests, but the destruction of the canal during the war that came out of this conflict. Even when it is a case of self-defense against an armed attack, the old obligation of proportionality of means ought to be observed. An all-out war in response to a raid grossly violates this rule.

On the other hand, in those cases when self-defense is justified, in some instances at least anticipatory self-defense ought to be morally tolerated. When military technology gives a great advantage to whomever strikes first, the potential victim does not have to wait until it is dead, or until the object of self-defense—political independence and territorial integrity—has been annihilated, before being morally able to defend itself. Clearly, anticipatory self-defense—preemptive war—can be even more of a source of self-serving claims than self-defense against an armed attack in progress. Walzer deals with the case of Israel's first strike in 1967. He justifies it even though he believes (rightly) that Nasser probably had no intention of striking first, but because he thinks that "states may use military force in the face of threats of war, whenever the failure to do so would seriously risk their territorial integrity or political independence."[10] I have mixed feelings on the matter. One could argue that this risk would have materialized only after the failure of all attempts to resolve the crisis (and get the Straits of Tiran reopened) by diplomatic means. But it is true that further delay might have put Israel in a more difficult military position. It is also true that Nasser's intentions were hard to assess at the time—when his rhetoric kept escalating. We thus always come back to the

central difficulties of *jus ad bellum:* each state's resort to
self-interpretation, and the political uncertainties of assessment. What are legitimate causes for nondefensive
wars? They must be important enough to be, if not
"community causes" in a world that is not (yet) a community, at least nonselfish causes (by which I do not mean, I
repeat, altruistic ones); ends that transcend the (evident)
interest of the initiating state, and that can be called
world order ends. Here we come across two very serious
and related problems. One is the relation between a
state's rights in international society and its domestic
moral foundations. The other is the contradiction between world order concerns. I have indicated previously
that an ethics of international relations ought to be an
ethics of self-restraint; but legitimizing force by arguing
that it is being used for a valid purpose of concern to all
states always threatens self-restraint. World order causes
give a dangerous license to crusaders and can become
pretexts for national expansion. One has to go through
cases quite carefully.

One purpose seems to me, on its face, unambigu-
ously valid: aid to a victim of armed external aggression.
(I insist on the words armed and external. External attack
can be more insidious and take the form of subversion; I
will deal with this later, along with the case of civil war.)
The preservation of the political independence and territorial integrity of states from armed attack is the cor-
nerstone of international society. As Hailé Selassié
warned the members of the League of Nations at the time
of Italy's invasion of Ethiopia, each one of them must fear
becoming "someone's Ethiopia" some day. It is this principle which not only justifies Britain and France's decision to go to war against Hitler after his invasion of
Poland, but makes their appeasement of Hitler in 1938
shameful: in order to "save" him from having to grab the

Sudetenland by force, Britain and France gave him what he wanted thus rewarding aggression. By declaring war in 1939, the British and French fought in the worst possible circumstances—having already lost all of eastern Europe, thrown the Soviets into the arms of the Germans, let the German army and air force grow. In the current case of Afghanistan, the Soviet argument according to which the Red Army intervened to protect a friendly government, at its request, against externally fostered subversion is obviously fake: the leader of that government was overthrown and killed, and the resistance met by the Soviets and their Afghan friends, even if (poorly) helped from the outside, is native. The Red Army's move of December 1979 is a case of aggression, as had been the invasion of Czechoslovakia in 1968. This is why, quite apart from the practical problems and grave risks, and from the issue of a political outcome, a decision by the United States to aid the victims of aggression in Afghanistan would not—it is the least one could say—be morally offensive.

Another case, which could be described as a consequence of the principle of resistance to aggression, is the recuperation of territory wrested by force, under the following conditions: when this territory is predominantly inhabited by members of the national community that lost it, when the loss was not consented to (I realize that many treaties, especially those concluded at the end of wars, are *diktats* and ratify the results of force, but there can be no social order without *pacta sunt servanda*), and when all other means of redress have been exhausted.

There are other cases of valid use of force about which there is a great deal of argument. They are instances of forceful intervention into the domestic affairs of states, when the domestic basis of their rights—the consent of the citizens—is obviously in trouble. The cases which Walzer approves are the use of force to help a nation achieve self-determination, when it is oppressed within the borders of a multiethnic state (the example he gives in his book, which sometimes takes refuge in history, is that of the Hungarians in 1848, but he has more recently extended this category to the blacks of South Africa)[11] counterintervention (if a state has intervened by force in the affairs of another, by supporting one faction in the civil war, it is legitimate to intervene on the other side not in order to win but to restore a certain kind of balance); and a traditional category, "humanitarian intervention," the use of force to put an end to particularly atrocious acts like genocide, large-scale massacres, deliberate famines, the enslavement of whole populations.

These cases go in different directions. Counter-intervention is actually aimed at restoring infringed sovereignty—the sovereignty of my neighbor has been dented by the intervention of another state in the civil war which rages over my neighbor's territory, and I try to restore its integrity by intervening on the other side, so that both sides struggling in that country will have a chance to fight it out evenly and the outcome will not be dictated by the first intervention. The other two cases—self-determination and humanitarian intervention—are very clearly exceptions to the principle of sovereignty, but exceptions in two different ways. Intervention for self-determination is an apparent exception to the international basis of the principle of sovereignty, but it goes to the roots of the domestic basis of that principle: a state is entitled to it as long as there is a presumption that it is the constitutional expression of a national community—of the will of its people to live together, to rule themselves, and not to be under foreign rule: as long as the principle of self-determination has been applied; otherwise the state is not the inhabitants' state, it is somebody else's

state, or the state of only one of the national communities
in it. The domestic root, in other words, is what could be
called the horizontal social contract, which gives rise not
just to a nation (a cultural reality and concept) but to a
nation-state (a political and legal construct and concept),
or to a voluntary federation of nations, with a nationality.[12] And therefore help to a secessionist movement derives from an individual's right to have a nationality of his
own. On the other hand, humanitarian intervention
goes, so to speak, above the principle of sovereignty. It
recognizes that there exist basic human rights, such as the
right to life, which transcend the limits of the state.
Hence the legitimacy of outside intervention in cases of
genocide, famine, etc.

These cases have been attacked from two very
different directions. Some authors have criticized Walzer
for having drawn too vast a list of possible interventions;
and some have criticized it for being too narrow, for not
allowing for enough just wars, so to speak. Walzer has
replied with great vigor and depth to the latter. I will
present my own view of this debate. Charles Beitz[13] has
asked why one should allow a state to intervene in a case
like Biafra, or in a case of national liberation from colonial rule, since the so-called right to self-determination
derives from the principle of nationality. This critic dis-
misses this principle by trying to refute John Stuart Mill's
two arguments on its behalf—that entities eligible to
claim self-determination are self-defining, and that self-
determination is the precondition of free representative
government. It is true that the problem of eligibility
(what is a nation?) is vexing, and that the connection
between self-determination and self-government is complex. But the grounds on which this critique stands in
order to desanctify, so to speak, the right to self-
determination are even more debatable than Mill's case:
it is the superior importance of social justice, on behalf of

which Beitz argues that self-determination cannot be justified merely when an overwhelming majority wants independence, but only when no great injustices would result for dissenting minorities, and the granting of independence would help reduce social injustice. It is true that a country which has achieved self-determination is sometimes as badly off afterward as before. Why then, asks Beitz, should its people be given the right to exchange the yoke of their former rulers for the yoke of their new, corrupt leaders? As I have said before, this view takes into account neither the importance of self-determination as a constitutive principle of international society (a fact Beitz might deem morally neutral, but international society needs such a principle, and surely social justice devoid of territorial bases is not a realistic alternative), nor the fact that for most people independence is a precondition of social justice. As Walzer points out in his reply, when there is no self-determination, whatever the flaws of the principle, or the difficulties of enforcing it, there is no fit at all between the government and the citizens.

Another criticism of Walzer that charges him with allowing too many interventions asks why counter-intervention should be deemed valid, in a civil war, against the "good guys," so to speak. If the other, prior foreign intervention was on the side of the "democratic or liberal forces of the majority," why should one "have the right to intervene on the side of the tyrannical government and its supporters merely to restore the original balance of forces?"[14] Walzer replies that "counter-interventions of this sort are justified without reference to the moral character of the parties . . . ; that kind of neutrality is a feature of all the rules of war; without it there could be no rules at all but only permissions addressed to the Forces of Good entitling them to do whatever is necessary to overcome their enemies."[15]

This criticism of an excessively neutral rule derives from the same conception that underlies the attack
on Walzer for having defined too narrow a list of legitimate interventions. It is charged that he should have
added a fourth category, the legitimacy of intervening by
force in order to establish or restore democracy in other
countries. In other words, if one vindicates interventions
for self-determination, why not authorize interventions
for self-government? Is it not a distinction without a
difference? If one denies the legitimacy of interventions
to establish democracy in tyrannical regimes, isn't one
actually saying that states have rights independent of the
consent of the governed? The argument which Walzer
uses to buttress his position is that of John Stuart Mill:
people fighting for freedom against their own government must win that fight themselves—the antipaternalist
argument. One cannot receive the right of self-
government from somebody else. The critics of Mill and
of Walzer reply with two arguments. One is categorical:
unfree illegitimate states should have no right of political
sovereignty. Furthermore—this is a utilitarian
consideration—modern governments have a formidable
power of repression, and the view of Mill that the rebels,
if they represent the will of the people, will always prevail
and therefore don't need external help has been made
totally wrong and irrelevant by modern techniques of
control.

My own argument will be complex, or, to use a
fashionable word, dialectic. First, I am very uneasy with
Mill's pronouncements. If a freedom fighter must "do
the job" himself, why should this apply to a battle against
a domestic tyrant and not to a struggle for self-
determination against an alien ruler? Walzer states that
Algerians would not like to be ridden of a dictatorship by
a wondrous Swedish chemical, and that the Sandinistas
never asked for military intervention because they

thought that they could achieve majority support and "wanted their own victory to build upon." Why would not the same reasoning apply to the black South Africans? If intervention on behalf of Biafra (or Hungary) is justified by the fact that a people that wants to secede cannot hope to "achieve majority support" outside their own region (a utilitarian calculation), why not provide outside help to a democratic force which government police methods prevent from mobilizing a latent but cowed majority?

Secondly, however, it must be recognized that there *is* a difference between the two kinds of cases. Walzer is on much stronger ground when, leaving Mill behind, he argues that all states rights are based on individual rights, but that individuals have two kinds of rights: the right to a state of their own—the horizontal contract already mentioned, which is the source of political obligation—and the right to political and civil liberty—the vertical tie which, within the state, binds the government to the people. The first right gives the people of the state a right against foreigners, who are unqualified to judge the fit between the people and its government. The second right is "meaningless" unless the state exists first: "as individuals need a home, so rights need a location." The violation of political and civil liberty justifies the citizens' resistance, but not the foreigners' intervention. International legitimacy depends on the presumption of fit. This presumption falls when the principle of self-determination has been clearly violated or suppressed. But once the nation-state, or the state based on a common willingness of citizens to be, say, French rather than German, citizens of Bangladesh not of Pakistan, is established, "the tyranny of established government gives rise to a right of revolution," not to a right of foreign intervention. There is, therefore, a "dual reference" for the doctrine of legitimacy. Internal legitimacy is "monistic" or singular—it depends on the presence of democratic institutions. International legitimacy is pluralistic—in the sense that a state can be a legitimate actor and subject of rights even if its government is illegitimate at home: "people have a right to a state within which their rights are violated."[16] Some might argue that if foreigners are not qualified to judge the fit between a government and its people, they should not judge whether the state is based on the principle of self-determination either. But it remains the case that the latter, and not the principle of democratic government, is constitutive of international society.

Thirdly, nevertheless, the distinction ought to be a low fence rather than a high barrier. On the one hand, a "radical" absence of fit can exist within a nation, when there is open warfare between the people and the government (cf. Somoza's or the Shah of Iran's last year). On the other, I would argue that in principle military non-intervention should be the rule not only in cases of people struggling for self-government as Walzer does, but also in cases of self-determination.

I recognize that defending the dogma of non-intervention exposes one to charges of amorality or immorality. Does it not amount to sanctifying the rights of states, even when their foundation violates what I have called the constitutive principle of international order? Since in practice the beneficiary of the states' rights is the regime, the government, does not non-intervention amount to supporting frequently illegitimate regimes—regimes deprived either of internal or both of internal and international legitimacy? We must, however, remember that we are dealing here with the problem of military force operating across borders, and that we are searching for a moral guideline. Now, for reasons given before, a utilitarian formulation—intervene militarily whenever the result would maximize happiness—really provides no guideline at all. A principle of legitimate

intervention in the cases of secession or national liberation runs into two objections. First, while the struggling
national community has not yet established its state, a
weaker version of Walzer's argument about the distinction between national and foreigners applies: foreign
intervention risks turning a struggle for national liberation into something quite different; "intervention is likely
to be unwelcome simply because it comes from outside".[17] Secondly, in a world of self-help, the impartiality
of the foreign sword is dubious: the proximate or façade
end of national liberation may conceal an ultimate end of
external domination. This is even more true in cases of
intervention against a tyrannical regime—in addition to
the arguments given by Walzer and grounded in his
analysis of state rights. If there were an impartial arbiter
capable of licensing legitimate interventions and of rul-
ing out biased ones, one might choose a different
guideline. But the need to consider likely consequences,
and their meaning not merely in individual cases, but for
international society as a whole, lead me, reluctantly, to
what may appear as a conservative and restrictive position. But remember two recent cases: Turkey invading
Cyprus in order to promote self-determination for the
Turkish minority there, and Somalia attacking Ethiopia
in order to wrest the Somali-populated Ogaden from
Addis Ababa's rule. The local and international reper-
cussions hardly support the case for military intervention. Given the small number of democracies, and the fog
that surrounds the claims to an application of the principle of self-determination, to allow military interventions
on behalf of either is a formula for generalized war and
hypocrisy.

However, and this is a fourth step, precisely because of my conviction that the international legitimacy
of states depends ultimately on the principle of national
self-determination, that the internal legitimacy of the

government depends on the principle of self-government, and that there are cosmopolitan concerns that transcend states rights, I propose to mitigate the rigors of the principle of non-intervention in the following ways. One, I will discuss in the next chapter the possibilities of an international policy of human rights, that is, nonmilitary efforts at dealing with deplorable internal conditions. Two, there is a difference between the effects of a crossing of borders by military forces, and the provision of military assistance to resisters fighting for national liberation or for liberation from tyranny: in the case of the Sandinistas Walzer himself mentions their asking for "equipment to match what the government was receiving or had received." Three, humanitarian interventions are precisely the kinds of interventions that become legitimate when the battle for self-determination or self-government entails large scale atrocities committed by a regime against the people. However, given the excesses of self-help and self-interpretation, it is only when the end of the intervention is the vindication of these principles that it is justified. One should distinguish between India's action in Bangladesh—aimed at dismembering Pakistan but also at liberating the population from the nightmare of Yahia Khan—or even the case of France in the Central African ex-Empire—removing Bokassa, previously supported by Paris, and assuring thereby the continuation of French influence, but also the end of genocide—from Vietnam's actions in Cambodia—which replaced Pol Pot's ghastly rule with quasi-conquest and famine; the case of Tanzania in Uganda is somewhere in between. The nature of the intervention, its scope, its length, and the means used have to be taken into account; not only the stated end, which is likely to be too saintly to be believed, or the real ends, likely to be ambiguous.

Finally, let us return to the case of counter-intervention in a civil war. My view is not identical with Walzer's. Let us assume that a foreign power has intervened on the side of a government that tries to crush either a rebellious community that fights for its independence, or an insurgency with deep roots and valid claims; in that case, counter-intervention is morally legitimate (whether it is politically wise or feasible—for instance in the case of the Eritreans, who battle an Ethiopian government helped by Soviets and the Cubans—is another matter). But if the foreign intervention is on the side of those who fight for self-government or self-determination, counter-intervention becomes more difficult to justify. Walzer's "neutral" rule is a bit too mechanical for comfort, and brings to mind the old saying that two wrongs do not make one right. If the foreign intervention is on the side of a rebellion that clearly cannot claim much support, and if it appears aimed at destroying a reasonably legitimate regime, or at replacing a nondemocratic but authentically national regime with a nondemocratic satellite regime, counter-intervention against subversion becomes legitimate again. In international affairs it is often difficult to distinguish between the second and the third hypotheses—once more, one must conclude that moral politics are contextual. I agree with Walzer that Vietnam falls in the second category (indeed, if one believes that North Vietnam was not a foreign power, and that the war was a civil war, the U.S. was not counter-intervening but intervening on the side of a government that failed "to meet the most minimal standards"[18]). But consensus on where real cases fit is even less likely than agreement on guidelines. This is why, even if there can be reasonable doubt as to the category into which the case fits, and even if it seems to be one in which counter-intervention is morally legitimate (many supporters of the American role in Vietnam would have argued that it fell into the third, not into the second category), a decisive judgment as to the morality of the counter-intervention is inseparable from a weighing of consequences. In the case of Vietnam, we were caught in a tragic dilemma: the observance of restraints, largely because of the risks of an extension of the war, doomed the American effort to failure, yet that effort condemned the local population to intense suffering; full victory would have required a morally and politically intolerable escalation of means and risks. Once again, we find the need to go beyond intentions, to a consideration of practical realities and likely effects.

The view I have presented clearly rules out two kinds of uses of force, and leaves a third one in the dark. The latter is the case of military intervention at the request of a friendly government—likely to be imperfect—that battles an attempted coup d'etat or a local faction not necessarily more representative or popular than itself (cf. the French and later the Libyans in Chad) or a very dubious secessionist movement (cf. the Shaba, ex-Katanga, province of Zaïre). Such interventions are valid in international law. Their moral validity is less obvious; there is no alternative to weighing the effects of preserving the status quo vs. the effects of its collapse (a calculation which is obviously plagued by the fact that domestic effects may be the opposite of external ones, and which is likely, given the state of the international contest, to favor intervention more often than not). There are two types of military ventures that are, however, clearly morally wrong. One consists of interventions by force against a legitimate revolutionary movement abroad—whether it is already in power (and especially when it came to power legally) or not quite yet. And yet this has been a recurrent policy of the United States: in Iran in 1953, in Guatemala in 1954, at the Bay of Pigs in 1961; it has been ardently pursued by Mr. Kissinger, in his vendetta against Mr. Allende in Chile, and it has again been advocated by him in the case of Nicaragua. The other kind of wrongful war is that which Robert W. Tucker has described as peculiarly American—the war whose origin is impeccable (self-defense) but whose goal becomes nothing less than the elimination of all wars in history—an end so ambitious that everything becomes permissible. This brings us to the problem of means.

Two kinds of issues must be distinguished: the morality of what Walzer calls the war convention—*jus in bello:* what is morally tolerable in war—and the morality of deterrence.

The very difficulty of defining nondistortable moral ends in a decentralized milieu suggests the importance of dealing with means usable in war. Let us consider first the use of nuclear weapons and then the conventional means. It is impossible to justify at all the morality of countercity nuclear war. Some may want to argue that the magnitude of the stakes might justify limited countercity warfare, as in some "scenarios"— exchange Birmingham, or Boston, against Kiev or Sverdlovsk—but these are not very believable, and even utilitarians might find it hard to assert that such "demonstrations" could improve general utility. It is this very critique of "mutual assured destruction," as well as its decreasing plausibility, and evidence of a different Soviet strategic doctrine, that has led several strategic thinkers to the notion of making nuclear war morally acceptable by advocating a counterforce nuclear war (limited or not). Destroying cities is bad, destroying military objectives with nuclear weapons is good. This position, taken by Paul Ramsey and Fred Iklé, and now by the U.S. government, strikes me as indefensible. The argument for it is that counterforce warfare will deter more because it is more credible. (The Russians cannot really believe that we will be ready to commit suicide by destroying all their cities. They will be more impressed by the combination of a more plausible threat with the residual risk of escalation, and the likelihood of collateral damage.) Also, counterforce nuclear war is deemed morally superior because it is a threat to do things much less horrid than city-busting: it aims at a most traditional aim of war, the destruction of the other side's forces. There is nothing horrible in destroying the enemy's silos; it is horrible to destroy his cities.

But there are enormous problems. One Ramsey himself recognizes is the certainty of what he calls "great collateral damage"; in other words, one would kill a few million people situated around the silos or the troop concentrations or the airports or the factories. Ramsey argues that it does not really matter because it is unintended. Needless to say, we go back to the meaninglessness of "unintended" when the unintended is known, inevitable, and accepted. Furthermore, there would be an enormous risk of escalation. Nobody knows, once one starts with military objectives, where one will end. If one believes that both the U.S. and the Soviet Union are in a situation of mutual invulnerability—neither side can destroy the other side's retaliatory forces in a first strike, nor cripple them so badly as to gain a decisive advantage— the search for counterforce warfare is either frivolous (why resort to nuclear weapons?) or criminal. If one believes that counterforce warfare is the answer to the new vulnerability of our (and soon of their) land-based missiles, one forgets either that a successful first strike against these represents a momentously hazardous cosmic roll of the dice; that even without one's panoply of land-based missiles enormous retaliatory forces remain available (so that a first strike against land-based missiles means taking enormous risks for dubious results); and that if one has already been struck by an attack on one's missiles, the most important available counterforce targets will have disappeared (the enemy's remaining land-based missiles won't wait to be destroyed in their silos), and hitting the other targets—ports, airfields, factories, communication centers, the enemy's political headquarters—will kill enough people to invite escalation, as well as to flunk the "moral test." Clearly the answer to vulnerability is either mobility, which restores (at what costs!) invulnerability, or the phasing out of land-based missiles. Counterforce scenarios suffer from implausibility. "Limited" counterforce targeting (an American specialty) is chimerical and more risky than conventional counterforce war; counterforce aimed at the enemy's strategic nuclear forces is both chimerical and destabilizing. The notion of counterforce nuclear warfare itself is ambiguous, and the underlying concept of a nuclear war of attrition is dubious. The gradual destruction of the enemy's military forces is not sufficient to give one "victory" as long as his countercity strike force is intact. For the ultimate threat in the nuclear age remains the menace of city destruction, and the practitioner of counterforce nuclear warfare can "win" only if it deters the loser from carrying out the supreme threat, thus sparing the "winner's" cities.[19] This is independent of the momentary military balance, since the ability to hit enemy cities exists whether one is superior or inferior in first-strike forces. Such is the meaning of the nuclear revolution. The relation of counterforce to countercity abilities is like the relation that non-violence á la Gandhi had to the threat that it might degenerate into violence if the other side did not yield.

Does this mean that one can never justly use nuclear weapons? I will give a forked answer. The use of nuclear weapons would be morally acceptable if one could invent nuclear weapons which do not produce any collateral damage and which can be used away from cities. The weapon exists. It is the neutron bomb, against which a great deal of indignation has been arrayed but which, strangely enough, fits all the canons of traditional just-war doctrine. It only kills soldiers, supposedly (if aimed at combatants); it does not destroy property, which has earned it the reputation of the perfect weapon for capitalist societies; and it has no diffuse radiation effects. From the old viewpoints of effectiveness, proportionality, and the double effect rule, it is a fine weapon. There is only one problem with it: once you start breaching the nuclear taboo, you do not know where you will stop; and you have to weigh this against all the charms of the neutron bomb. The line which separates conventional from nuclear war has been meticulously preserved since 1945. Can we be sure statesmen will remain in full control once the taboo has been broken even at the lowest level? My conclusion is that I would not advocate the use of nuclear weapons on ethical grounds—no great surprise, I suppose. What neutron bombs can do, we must seek nonnuclear weapons for.

On traditional warfare, the most exacting attempt at defining limits and at preserving ways of "fighting well," the most eloquent defense of the view that a good cause does not justify all-out war, is Michael Walzer's book. If I do not go into details here, it is because I agree with many of his prescriptions (I will only express my main reservations). He tries to find a compromise between absolutist and utilitarian positions; it amounts to a kind of utilitarian plus, or absolute morality minus. The criterion which he applies to various categories of conventional warfare he describes as "Do justice unless the heavens are ready to fall." His aim is the protection of the lives and liberty of all those who have not surrendered or lost these rights (he considers that the soldiers who do the fighting have). Since the foundation of the state is the defense of these rights, it has to respect them even in war; and a state has to respect the rights of citizens of the enemy state, because these rights, while *enforced* in and through the state, and also the groups below the state in which many of these rights are exercised (and in which "the citizen is safer . . . from bureaucratic neglect or abuse"[20]) do not disappear when the state is defeated or destroyed, any more than they do in the case of stateless people cast off by a state. In other words, Walzer tries to save the notion, familiar to eighteenth-century theorists, that war is a contest of states, not of people. He starts therefore with the principle of noncombatant immunity, and he wants it to be respected—but not quite absolutely. Utilitarianism is reintroduced only in what he calls a supreme emergency. Where there is no supreme emergency, the principle of non-combatant immunity should stick; it is only when one has one's back to the wall, as the British did in the fall of 1940, that exceptions ought to be allowed. Walzer's formula is a kind of compromise between the absolutism of a Thomas Nagel, who would allow hostile treatment of a person only if "justified in terms of something *about that person* which makes the treatment appropriate"[21]—but recognizes "the utilitarian cost of refusing to adopt a prohibited course" such as massacre, and the utilitarianism of a R. B. Brandt, who deems a military action permissible "only if the utility . . . of victory to all concerned, multiplied by the increase of its probability if the action is executed, on the evidence . . . is greater than the possible disutility of the action to both sides multiplied by its probability,"[22] a calculation I would not envy any field commander for having to make before his decision. Walzer realizes that an absolute absolutist stand, so to speak, will not be observable by statesmen and military leaders, precisely because it could lead to intolerable consequences for the national *and* the general interest. But he is also wary of the "sliding scale" of utilitarianism, which "enables soldiers to do terrible things and to defend ... the terrible things they do."[23]

There are of course a number of problems with

Walzer's principle and applications. One is the difficulty of drawing a clear line between combatants and non-combatants. On the one hand, modern industrial war turns those civilians "who make what (soldiers) need to fight"[24] into military targets assimilated, in their factories, to the combatants. On the other hand, the contrast drawn by Walzer between civilians, on behalf of whom he proposes tightening and revising the double effect rule (so that the forseeable evil shall be minimized), and soldiers, who do the fighting and are deemed to have lost the rights of civilians, and gained only rights as combatants and potential war prisoners, is a bit strained. The existing laws of war, and current practices, allow or entail the use of ghastly weapons, and it is hard to argue that it makes no difference whether the agents of the state are killed in a humane or in an inhumane way—especially since, as Walzer admits, soldiers are far from all being volunteers. The rights of soldiers as combatants and prisoners need to be strengthened also, and a major international effort at defining and barring what might be called sadistic or terroristic weapons is a moral duty.

Secondly, there are obvious difficulties in applying the principle of supreme emergency. Will not any statesman convinced of the importance of his cause be tempted to plead acute necessity sooner rather than later? Will not the information at his disposal be anything but (to use Brandt's formulation) "reasonably solid, considering the stakes"? How does one know when the supreme emergency has ended? Walzer, writing thirty-five years later, says that it was morally acceptable for the British to bomb German cities in 1940 because that appeared to be the only chance for the British to survive and given the justice of their cause, but it was no longer acceptable in 1942–45, because the supreme emergency had passed. This is an ex post argument; it is hard to make the case that (at the time, in a world of self-help) the

British should have known it. After all, in 1942 the Germans were still all over Russia. And if supreme emergency is defined as the military situation multiplied by the stakes, is Walzer suggesting that a state that fights an unjust war can never invoke extreme necessity?

A third difficulty is pointed out by a possible utilitarian counterattack against the principle itself, which he does not take sufficiently into account. If I were a utilitarian reading Michael Walzer's rather saintly book, I would make the following two points. One is that the imperative of noncombatant immunity, except in supreme emergency, risks prolonging the evil of war. Why should not one's precept be that the war ought to brought to the fastest possible end even if it is a fairly bloody one? This is not a Shermanesque (or, says Walzer—wrongly—Clausewitzian) idea of limitlessness, but the idea that—in a just war—the limit in time provided by quick victory is preferable to the uncertainties and prolongations Walzer's principle may entail. We have often heard that argument made by proponents of an all-out effort during the Vietnam war; the argument, of course, was also made about the dropping of the atomic bomb on Hiroshima. Walzer deals with it by declaring the defense of the destruction of Hiroshima either on utilitarian grounds (it saved more lives than it destroyed) or on grounds of supreme emergency unacceptable, because we had trapped ourselves by our war aims. If we had not requested unconditional surrender, which implied an occupation of Japan—a defeat of Japan on the ground—we would not have had to throw the bomb in order to kill fewer Japanese than we would lose men in landing there. This is true, but one does not always have that argument—Walzer points out himself that unconditional surrender was justified in the case of Germany. If it was justified in the case of Germany (as I also believe), and if one could prove that massive bombings would hasten the defeat of Nazism by weakening the morale of the population, why should one not resort to them? Secondly, the utilitarian counterattack argues not only that Walzer's principle risk prolonging evil, but that it sometimes also risks making the victory of evil much easier. What if the enemy does not play by the same rules? Does one have to wait until one is in dire straits before retaliating in kind? This problem is particularly acute in the case of guerrilla wars. Walzer applies his principle to them—one should fight guerrillas with due respect for the principle of noncombatant immunity. But guerrilla war is both a war fought for the control of the population's "hearts and minds," and a war in which the distinction between soldiers and civilians gets especially blurred. Won't Walzer's rule mean fighting with a hand tied behind one's back? He replies, in effect, that if one cannot win that way one does not deserve to win. But this is based on the very optimistic assumption that by fighting well in a good cause, one is likely to win; and that if one loses, it means that one's cause or methods were wrong.

The truth of the matter is that we are in a dilemma. Walzer is right in distrusting utilitarian calculations. Take the case of obliteration bombings: in the case of Nazi Germany, they happened, almost until the end, not to destroy the morale of the population (this was not true in Italy). If this had been known, a utilitarian would have had to take the same position as a defender of noncombatant immunity; but since it could not be known at the time of the fateful decision to bomb civilians, utilitarianism would have had to be based on a guess, most likely on a wishful guess that would have turned out both wrong and murderous. It is precisely because each side is likely to be sure of the justice of its cause (and tempted therefore to do all it can to win fast), and because one cannot be sure that there is indeed a clear choice between a mitigated but endless horror, and a horrible but quick end—because one cannot be sure that a swift devastating blow will do the trick (remember 1914, and the Schlieffen plan)—that the utilitarian counterattack is not decisive, quite apart from the moral revulsion believers in individual rights feel when massacre becomes a subject of calculations of usefulness. But the problem with Walzer's rules is that they assume a stoic and somewhat unpolitical determination of just statesmen to sacrifice to the duty of fighting well the opportunities provided by modern technology and to accept terrible risks for their cause by leaving their adversary—for instance in guerrilla war—with a monopoly on terror and a relative immunity from counterblows.

There is something heroic in the effort to inject morality in the Hobbesian situation par excellence—when states, locked in war, squirm on the floor of survival. It is good to remind statesmen that the ends do not justify all means, that restraints should be observed even in an angry war, that humanity must somehow be preserved. And there have been in the postwar world conflicts fought with conventional weapons, in which civilians have been spared, although perhaps for prudential reasons more than because of a sense of duty (the result is the same); for instance in the Arab-Israeli wars of 1956, 1967, 1973. But guerrilla wars have been particularly atrocious, and the limits observed in the Middle East may not be easy to generalize (or to perpetuate even there). The combination of technological means of mass destruction and of inexpiable conflicts makes the question a moral *jus in bello* something of a Sisyphean task. We are in what Thomas Nagel calls "a moral blind alley."

Given the endless temptations of self-help in the interpretation of ends, and the difficulty of fighting contemporary wars in ways that are morally satisfying, the moral task of restraining the use of force cannot be exhausted by the advocacy of limits on ends and means.

War prevention is a moral duty. We all know, having read Clausewitz, that war ought to be subordinated to political ends and moderated by them. But in a century of immoderate politics and terrible means, Clausewitz' precepts, like those of Walzer (who compares strategy and morality) may remain pious hopes. The attempt to moralize interstate conflict cannot consist only of legal and ethical rules for or in war; it is inseparable from the political game, if the latter aims at avoiding war or at creating (as in the Middle East) conditions that will incite leaders to observe restraints out of self-interest. Once again we find that we should not pose the problem of ethics and international affairs as a problem of morality vs. politics (even though political judgments often violate the ethical standards I have tried to suggest). It is through the right kind of politics that some moral restraints can become observed and practicable. Today, in many instances, morality requires not only a *jus in bello* and a *jus ad bellum,* but a *jus* or rather a praxis—*ante et contra bellum.*

This brings us back to the troubling question of the morality of nuclear deterrence—the attempt to preserve peace by the threat of resorting to nuclear weapons if one is attacked. (Let us remember that, as a means of avoiding war, it has been of only partial effectiveness: it has not prevented a host of violent conflicts, and may have enhanced the quest for proxy wars, guerrilla wars, subversive actions, etc. as ways of using force without risking nuclear destruction). In the (so far vast) domain in which it has been effective (there have been neither nuclear wars nor large-scale conventional wars among states armed with nuclear weapons) can it also be deemed moral? Deterrence can be morally defended, with reservations, at two levels—the level of intentions and the level of consequences. In a way, self-defense and deterrence are quite comparable. In an ideal world where everybody would be good, one would not have to defend oneself, and one would not have to deter anybody. Still, the end of deterrence is *not* to have to execute the evil threat of total destruction; even though deterrence consists in threatening to kill innocents, which is indeed bad, the purpose of making the threat—the ultimate purpose—is not to have to do so. At the level of consequences, deterrence is commendable as long as it is credible (which is a big if), as long as it does succeed in maintaining peace. It may save a small state, or even a great power, armed with nuclear weapons to deter an aggressor, from having to surrender to it, or from being tempted to do so. No nuclear state which faces another nuclear power can indulge in hubris of its own; in other words, these weapons serve as a restraint on one's own ambitions or inclinations. Last but not least, the effectiveness of nuclear deterrence so far in reducing the level of wars among the nuclear powers is itself morally commendable. The good thing about deterrence, in terms of consequences, is that it saves us (partly) from Clausewitz: certain kinds of war are no longer the continuation of politics by other means.

However, there are limits. One has to do with credibility. Nuclear deterrence—especially extended deterrence, covering allies—is credible only for very high stakes, and credibility requires large armaments. Moreover, the effectiveness of deterrence has also, until now, been connected to its being mutual; in other words, would war, conventional or nuclear, be averted if a country acquired nuclear weapons against a neighbor which does not have them, or in the case of two nuclear states whose deterrents are very vulnerable, so that the acquisition of nuclear weapons could be an incentive to preventive war? This is the risk to which nuclear proliferation beyond the current nuclear states exposes mankind. To assume, as does Kenneth Waltz,[25] that the balance of terror that exists between Washington and Moscow, or even between Moscow and Peking, will be reproduced in future cases, or that eventual nuclear conflicts between lesser powers (or the prospect of such conflicts) would not affect the superpowers or risk exacerbating their contest is highly panglossian.

Defenders of the morality of nuclear deterrence point at consequences so far. Critics point to the disastrous effects should it fail. These critics fall into two categories. One is that of nuclear disarmers. Not only are they unlikely to be heeded but—since we have to weigh consequences—can one be sure that a world without nuclear weapons would not be much more bellicose, and that the superpowers would observe the same restraints they have preserved so far? The other category deserves being taken more seriously because it is more influential. It is made of those who argue that a failure of deterrence would be catastrophic only if it led to all-out countercity warfare—not if one's "deterrent posture" were one of counterforce. Countercity deterrence is not credible any more, and morally horrendous effects would follow from its (possible) failure. Moreover, a country that has put all its eggs in the countercity basket exposes itself to blackmail—the adversary can aim at "escalation dominance" and try to force that country into an unsavory choice between holocaust and capitulation. I have dealt earlier with the morality of counterforce. Two things need to be added here. If counterforce deterrence is credible, is it not because of the certainty of huge collateral damage and the risk of escalation? And if one begins to think in terms of winning a nuclear war, does one not thereby diminish the strength of the nuclear taboo, does one not actually weaken deterrence and make nuclear war—even large-scale conventional war—more rather than less likely?

It remains true that the credibility of countercity deterrence is limited to great stakes and that it may be insufficient to deter nonnuclear attacks even on important allies or vital stakes abroad. Conversely, when the stakes are great, its plausibility must be enhanced by the existence of a continuum of weapons—conventional, tactical nuclear, counterforce; but when the stakes are low, to try to protect them through nuclear deterrence of any kind is a morally and politically odious bluff. And it is true that should deterrence fail any use of strategic nuclear weapons would be disastrous. This suggests that a failure of nuclear deterrence to deter war ought not to doom a state to resort to such weapons: it must have alternative strategies available. It is also true that the evolution of technology strengthens the advantage of whoever strikes first. But the answer ought to be sought, not in every nuclear power striving for that advantage, and seeking greater invulnerability than its rivals, but in a quest for arms control capable of restoring some stability and of enforcing a principle of equal security—or equal vulnerability even after having struck first.[26]

CITIZENS AND THE MORALITY OF WAR

So far we have only dealt with the dilemmas of the statesmen. There are problems for the citizens as well. The antinomies described by Kant and Rousseau weigh most heavily on citizens of nontotalitarian countries. Those in totalitarian ones have, so to speak, much less of an opportunity to be morally torn between country and humanity. But it is for all citizens of countries at war that the old dilemmas have been worsened in the twentieth century. They have been universalized, and they have been deepened. They have been universalized because modern war mobilizes whole populations and increases enormously the state's capacity—already considerable in peacetime—to compel its citizens. This is what the draft does, this is what propaganda tries to accomplish. How then can the citizen control decisions that will affect his life? Moreover, much of international relations, in an age of deterrence especially, becomes a preparation or a substitute for war. In one's daily peacetime life, one is already affected by it; there are boycotts of hostile countries, travel limitations, and vast defense establishments. There are states living in a state of siege, like Israel, or in a state of endless war, like Vietnam. And the old dilemmas have also been deepened, because of what modern means of warfare do to the civilians, to the average citizens. They get killed because the destruction of their morale is part of the search for effectiveness. The principle of noncombatant immunity has been violated by everybody, because in modern warfare everybody can be deemed a combatant except infants—unless one accepts the distinctions between types of civilian activity Walzer wants to preserve. In guerrilla wars even children of twelve can be combatants, and how does one know who is and who is not? Defoliants, saturation bombings, the taking of hostages, and torture have devasted civilian lives. The dilemmas have also been deepened because not only in warfare, but in daily international politics citizens become engaged in tests of respective conceptions of life. In the modern state one's loyalties are under strain: to what extent does one's allegiance to the nation obliterate not only one's sense of belonging to the human race, but one's intranational allegiance to a party, to a class, to an ethnic group, or one's supranational allegiance (such as to the Jewish people, or to Islam—or to science)?

Citizens face two problems: the problem of obedience and the problem of national loyalty. The problem of obedience is specifically the soldier's problem, and the problem of national loyalty is the average citizen's problem.

Two questions can be asked about the soldiers.[27]

The first problem is posed in almost every modern war, and especially in wars of counterguerrilla activity, antisubversion, pacification, etc. Can one really distinguish between what is militarily "required" by the daily military operations, and the commission of war crimes like My Lai or like the dropping of bombs from an overloaded helicopter on obviously peaceful peasants? Can one say that these were indeed totally unnecessary, and that therefore whoever was in command that day is clearly guilty? Or aren't wars of that sort almost necessarily going to lead to war crimes, almost by their essence, because of the obliteration of any clear distinction between combatants and non-combatants?

Because of the weapons used in modern war, if you are dealing with a large-scale conventional war of the Korean kind—and the Korean war after all was smaller than World War II—there may be massive violations of all kinds of legal regulations on means. If you are dealing with a war like the Vietnamese or Algerian wars, almost by definition the attempt to control an uncertain civilian population will involve not only violations of the rules on the means of war, but, even more, violations of the provisions that are supposed to protect the civilians.

In that sense, one can assert that this kind of a war or perhaps all modern war in its full technological dimensions leads inevitably to war crimes, and that one has only the choice between abstaining from war altogether or committing war crimes more or less on a massive scale. One can still argue about the more or the less; one can make a case for "less" being better than "more," and for a duty to fight with the maximum of restraint, but it will be inevitably a delicate distinction, and one many statesmen and soldiers will resist.

The second problem has to do with the people who ought to be deemed responsible or punished for war crimes. Whether one is dealing with localized events like

My Lai, which are easily identified, or with the massive killing which is really the sum total of all the My Lai's, we are faced much more with a political and moral than with a legal issue. One can always establish that the Calleys of this world did what they should not have done, that they had—as indeed I think they had—a certain freedom to interpret orders, or to understand what was said to them. But then they come back to their judges, or else their defenders in the press come back to us, and say, "Yes, but they interpreted orders in a certain way because they knew that this was part of the accepted policy. It was, for instance, an accepted fact that when dealing with civilians of any age and of whom one didn't know whether they were really civilians or disguised combatants, security required that one not expose oneself too much; and this might have entailed indiscriminate killings."

Can the soldier, when he is given the order to drop bombs on innocent civilians, or to kill hostages, or to torture a prisoner, excuse himself from criminal responsibility by pleading that he was just following a policy or obeying orders, and that the responsibility belongs to his superiors (all the way to the Chief Executive)? Or can he only avoid criminal responsibility by taking upon himself the right to break his bond of loyalty to the state? Passing the buck or revolting: this was the dilemma faced by the bombing crews of World War II. (Michael Walzer does not discuss their case in his book.) The principle he suggests, following J. Glenn Gray, is that the more one can do to resist such orders—which means the more one is a soldier of a democracy—the more one is obliged to do. But is this likely to be effective? Not only are there mighty external pressures for compliance that weigh on the soldiers, but the internal conviction that one fights for a just cause is likely to offset some moral scruples; what Robert Lifton calls "psychic numbing" operates.

The problem of national loyalty is different. I am

thinking of the many cases of collaboration and treason in the world wars. What happens to the national bond of allegiance where there is, as in the France of 1940, a kind of ideological dissolution of the state, which makes some citizens sympathize with the enemy's philosophy and values? Or when there are conflicting conceptions of the requirements of patriotism, as existed in many countries of Nazi-occupied Europe? This is almost the opposite of the soldiers' problem—the latter results from the existence of a strong military hierarchy, which squeezes the soldier in the awful dilemma of either becoming an automaton by obedience, or else breaking the hierarchy if he rebels. The citizens' problem results rather from the collapse of the normal hierarchy in an ideologically torn or ideologically evil state.

Are there any possible answers? In the case of the soldiers' obedience, one must make one important distinction. There are, in modern as in past warfare, many individualized crimes, battlefield crimes committed by individual soldiers or small groups of soldiers for which their authors must take individual responsibility. There ought to be a criminal sanction of the guilty parties, and of those commanders of whom one can show that they gave orders that were criminal, or failed to prevent or sanction crimes of which they were not unaware. Battlefield crimes are essentially deliberate acts, individual violations traceable to specific persons who chose to exceed those legal and moral limits that ought to be observed even in modern war. The revolt against committing such acts is a perfectly legitimate revolt. The best example would be something like My Lai.

However, there is another category of acts which are much more problematic. They are either also illegal (like massive transfers of population or free-fire zones) or in a kind of legal no-man's-land (like the bombing of military targets on such a scale that huge civilian casualties are unavoidable). These acts result not from individual outrages, but from collective decisions. One could argue that battlefield crimes—although they can also be seen as a collapse of individual self-restraint—are nevertheless essentially choices for evil. The other kinds of acts—which can, of course, be seen as decisions for injury and pain—are, however, essentially failures to observe strategic self-restraint, all-too-easy capitulations to the mad momentum of technology, or to the "psycho-logic" of counter-insurgency. These are failures of policy, committed on a large scale in both world wars. (To be sure, such grand failures can be seen as encouraging, almost as authorizing smaller, localized atrocities. But the latter, alas, existed long before modern war and will probably persist even if leaders made a successful effort in their policies and strategies to define and apply a modern equivalent of the just war doctrine.) Many of the modern crimes of war, like the anonymous dropping of millions of tons of bombs on cities are really collective crimes—very different from a platoon going berserk and shooting everybody in a village. The acts in this second category are collective atrocities made easier or more justifiable by the nature of modern war. This makes individual responsibility much more diluted and individual revolt much more difficult. Can one member of a bombing crew really claim that he wants to have clean hands, when the responsibility for the dirt is collective—a decision which comes from on high, which has been approved at every level?

Here, individual, criminal responsibility gives way to collective, political responsibility. There is no reason for the average citizen to feel responsible for the first kinds of crimes (except insofar as any man feels responsible, so to speak, for Cain). But there are reasons why citizens, especially in democratic countries, and especially in the so-called informed public should feel responsible for allowing their leaders to let the imperative of victory, or the excuse of military necessity, override all other considerations—even when the citizens have reasons to believe that the leaders have deceived them by promising peace. This is why, insofar as the second category is concerned, when it comes to the political leadership and top military command, the best thing one can do is, if not to purge them (partly because of the truth in Malraux' epigram—there are two ways of destroying a country, one is physical destruction, the other consists in forcing it to repudiate its own freely chosen leaders; partly because legal purges have one moral drawback: they provide one with easy scapegoats), at least to retire them. And when one retires them, it is necessary, for the lawyers, moralists, and politicians who argue for these sanctions, to be and to make clear that it is not only the fault of those political or army leaders, and that the public has to be made aware of its own responsibilities. For citizens have a tendency to take refuge in the "banality of evil." And the very fact that there is a collective responsibility for the failure to examine the consequences of national policy should serve as an argument for amnesty to the individuals whose consciences rebelled against committing those kinds of collectivized crimes.

This brings one to the problem of the citizens' loyalty. The key question which should be asked in each of the instances of torment with which history has provided us recently is: What will be the effect, for my nation, of my conception of loyalty? One can make a very convincing distinction between pro-Nazi collaborationists and fascists in occupied France, whose conception of France or of ideological loyalty would have led to the enslavement of France to Nazism, and the German plotters against Hitler, who may have looked like traitors to Hitler, but who, if they had succeeded, would have at least succeeded in saving the honor of Germany; even though the two cases look comparable, they are not. One was a betrayal of the nation, on behalf of another nation or of the (temporary) victor's ideology. The other was the repudiation of a regime, whose behavior was bringing the nation to ruin and shame.

Ultimately one comes back to the question of individual conscience. Each individual has the right to refuse blind obedience or blind national loyalty under certain conditions—such as the German revolt against Hitler, or the case of soldiers who refuse to carry out criminal acts. A citizen convinced that his government is waging an unjust war, because it is being fought for morally intolerable ends and with morally outrageous means, ought to have a right to conscientious objection, and there may well be a "duty to disobey" if this right is not granted. Yet what state is willing to grant to all citizens, especially in emergencies, the right to judge the state's acts? However well one may argue that coercion and punishments destroy the foundations of pluralism, the risks of individual sovereignty for national cohesion are real, and self-help can be abused by the individual as well as by the state. When citizens or soldiers revolt for reasons of individual conscience, there is no way of denying that they will be seen by their fellow soldiers or their fellow citizens as breaking the bond of citizenship; however unfair this may be, they must be willing to pay a price. Those who take those rather fateful decisions cannot expect to be recognized as heroes and to be rewarded for it—since this would put to shame the vast majority who obey orders or remain sheepishly loyal. In this respect, as in the other realms of force, there are no easy solutions. There are no fully satisfying precepts, and even the least objectionable are open to distortions and deviations. All I could do was indicate a few signposts and repeat that since they do not allow for simple and automatic applications, they cannot save statesmen, soldiers, and citizens from the duty of moral assessment and choice in concrete cases.

I have stated, in the first chapter, that whenever states are closest to the pole of enmity, and struggling for survival and security, the opportunities for a non-Machiavellian morality will be poor. Logically, moral restraints are easier to preserve when the stakes are lower, when the states in conflict still have mixed interests—but should states resort to force at all for low stakes? As long as they keep using force, it is the duty of those of us who are not statesmen to remind leaders that they must think of the peace that will follow explosions of enmity, and that it is their duty to act in such a way that even if these explosions cannot be avoided, both the ends and the means will stay limited—so that the rest of us can preserve as many of our rights, and as much of our happiness, as is possible when our lives are shaped by those cold monsters, the states.[28]

~~~ 3 ~~~

The Promotion of Human Rights

WHAT ARE HUMAN RIGHTS?

*W*HEN ONE LOOKS at the problem of human rights, one finds the most acute example of all the incompatibilities between ethics and international politics, for the reasons mentioned in the first chapter. The structure of the international milieu which limits opportunities for moral action, the conflicts of value systems which result in very sharp disagreements on conceptions of human rights and on priorities, the difficulties of assessment and evaluation are all manifest here and lead repeatedly either to failure, or to confrontation, or to distorted uses of the human rights issues for purposes of political warfare at home or abroad.

It is also the most acute example of the clash between an ethics of imperatives and an ethics of consequences. In the matter of human rights, absolutes are largely or frequently counterproductive; on the other hand, an ethics of consequences is not very satisfactory either, because the effects of one's moves in this realm are extremely uncertain and often quite poor. Finally, this is one of the best examples of the collision between man as a citizen of his national community and what could be called an incipient cosmopolitanism, or man as a world citizen. When we deal with human rights, we are in the typical problem of the in-between—moving toward Kant's notion of cosmopolitan law, yet held back by the

95

fact that the chief actors in world affairs are the states, frequent violators of human rights.[1] It is therefore not surprising that a number of distinguished writers have thrown up their hands: "if our government should set out to pursue moral purposes in foreign policy, on what would it base itself? ... Are we to assume that it ... knows what is right and wrong, has imparted this knowledge to the people at large, and obtained their mandate to proceed to bring about the triumph of what is right, on a global scale?"[2]

I will start by examining the nature of the problem: What are human rights, and what are the pros and cons of a human rights policy? Then I will suggest what can be done about it. In dealing with the nature of the problem, the emphasis will not be specifically or primarily on the American human rights policy of the last few years, although for obvious reasons it provides probably the best example of all the difficulties and pitfalls.

When we ask: What are human rights, we have to review a number of subjects: first, a number of philosophical discussions on the nature and origins of human rights, next the question of what rights, and last, the status of these rights.

The philosophical discussions about the nature and origins of human rights are learned, complex, and fascinating; it can certainly be argued that before a statesman decides to make a national goal of their promotion he should have a firm moral theory about their essence and their foundations. But much of the literature has a tendency to overcomplicate what is already a formidably difficult subject. On the nature of rights, the most appealing notion is Maurice Cranston's idea of just entitlements.[3] If one is lucky and lives in the right kind of state, human rights can be positive rights, rights that people actually enjoy, but when one talks about human rights one ordinarily refers to rights which one can claim—not legally but morally—even when they are not positive rights. They belong, as Cranston puts it, to the category of what ought to be and not just to the category of what is. We are in the normative domain. Also relevant is the notion that when one refers to human rights, one mentions something which is a little stronger than ordinary rights: something that cannot be defeated by "an appeal to any of the routine goals of political administration, but only by a goal of special cogency," in Ronald Dworkin's phrase.[4] Another philosopher worth mentioning is Thomas Scanlon, with his remark (which is historically correct) that human rights developed as responses to specific threats, and are essentially demands on social and political institutions.[5]

If one moves to the origins of human rights, one has to distinguish between historical origins and philosophical foundations. Historically, they are inseparable from the development of the modern state, from secularization, from the evolution from status to contract in the West; also, they are inseparable from the extension of Western forms of government and constitutional systems all over the world. In that respect, the UN Charter is an interesting document, since it was adopted by all the nations and mentions the promotion of universal respect for and observance of human rights among its central purposes.

Philosophically, as usual, there is no agreement on the foundations. None of those mentioned is likely to be entirely satisfactory to everyone. One foundation is the Lockean theory: human rights are natural rights derived from the Law of Nature, a law of reason that imposes constraints on what individuals can do to one another, and protects the life, liberty, and possessions of equal and independent human beings. Such rights are inherent and inalienable. It has been objected that this theory cannot serve as a foundation for many of the rights which are now recognized as human rights, either because inalienability is a culture-bound Western concept,[6] or because the notion of natural rights implies that they must be both universally valid and belong to individuals (which is not the case of many of the rights proclaimed by current international agreements). But that would be true only in a Protestant perspective, not, for instance, in a Catholic one, in which rights belong to individuals in communities, and in which there is a difference between the individual and the person. The main problem with the natural rights foundation is that not everybody accepts the natural law tradition, even secularized.

A second possible foundation is not the Lockean but the Humean one: human rights derive directly from man's humanity and sociability. The problem with this is that it is pretty vague. One knows just by looking at a variety of societies that humanity and sociability are compatible with all kinds of behavior, not all of which are very attractive. A more recent idea is that human rights are "entitlements to the satisfaction of various human interests that would be guaranteed to members of the group by principles of social justice appropriate to the group."[7] This is not a satisfactory answer, for it raises but fails to answer the next question: Where do those principles of justice come from? If they are no more than principles which "express the conditions under which social institutions may be regarded as morally legitimate" in a group, and are related to the distribution of social benefits and burdens, aren't we relativizing and particularizing human rights *ad infinitum,* and moving from the natural law extreme to the other—to what might be called the anthropological—extreme? I am afraid that we will have to leave the question of philosophical foundations hanging in the air—not because there are no coherent moral theories from which conceptions of human rights derive, but because no single theory is universally accepted. For our purposes, it is enough to know that there is universal recognition of the *idea* of human rights—and disagreement about practically everything related to them.

This becomes obvious when we move to the central problem: What rights? It has to be divided into several questions: Whose rights? And what is their substance?

Concerning "whose rights," there are obviously different traditions. In the Western tradition we talk about the rights of individuals; the typical human right is the liberty of the person; the first of the great postwar documents, the Universal Declaration of Human Rights of 1948 is strikingly Western; it lists exclusively the rights of individuals. However, even in the West, over the last century, there has been increasing recognition of rights which are assumed to belong not to individuals but to specific groups—unions, minorities, women, national liberation movements, states. This culminated in the two United Nations covenants of 1966. The first article in each of them consecrates the peoples' right to self-determination. (It carefully avoids defining "peoples" for a very good reason: it could not have succeeded.) This marks quite an evolution from the earlier declaration. But this debate, which fills so many pages, on whether human rights are necessarily rights of individuals or can also be rights of groups or communal rights is perfectly absurd: in *both* cases we are dealing with the rights of individuals; individuals exist both as human beings—I was going to say as abstractions, as universals, as persons endowed with reason, feelings, and a moral instinct—and as members of a variety of collectivities whose own existence is indispensable to the individuals' fulfillment. We may emphasize either the general or the particular, the abstract or the concrete; but neither makes full sense without the other.

The next question has also been the cause of a

great battle. What substantive rights can individuals morally claim? There is a noisy debate between those who believe in the superior status of personal, civil, and political rights on one hand, and those who believe in the equal or even superior importance of economic and social rights. There are two United Nations covenants, one for each group. Those who believe in the superior status of personal, civil, and political rights point out that they are all rights against the state, rights which limit the state and require its abstention, and that they are therefore, so to speak, cost-free. No state, at whatever level of development, has really any excuse for not granting them, precisely because this requires mere abstention—whereas the granting of economic and social rights may well be beyond the capacity of many governments (full employment, for instance).[8] As one of the defenders of this particular tradition puts it, rather excessively, it is only when these rights are secured that one can even begin to address economic and social needs.[9] Needless to say, this is exactly the opposite of what a good Marxist would say—and even many people—including Rawls—who are not Marxists, yet who believe that political, civil, and personal rights are mere empty forms if one has not done something first about the economic and the social needs of individuals and peoples. This is the view of many Third World experts and lawyers, and much of the Left in the West. In other words, one needs a floor providing for basic human needs before one can begin to talk about freedom from the state or freedom to participate in the state.

How deep is the split? How important is this debate? It is politically significant; intellectually, one should beware of turning nuances into abysses. The separation between the two kinds of rights has been considerably exaggerated; the distinction is much less deep than many of the arguments in the literature suggest. Both categories of rights, the civil and political as well as the economic and social ones, require from the state a mix of abstention and action. Each one of them, whether it is called a political right or an economic one, demands in effect that the state stop or refrain from doing certain things, *and* provide certain things. To take the case of one of the supposedly archetypical personal or political rights, the right to a fair trial requires that the state set up positive institutions. And, to take an almost archetypically economic right, the right to join unions, it requires that the state abstain from doing what it does in so many nations of the present world, which is interfere in the labor field so as to prevent the organized expression of grievances. If one starts with the notion of personal integrity as the essence of human rights, clearly it requires both freedom from torture, from arbitrary imprisonment, from slavery (which are all civil and political rights), and freedom from famine as well as the existence of adequate health conditions (which are economic and social ones). As one student of the matter has put it,[10] all human rights entail three correlative duties from the state: first, the duty to forbear from depriving people of those rights; second, the duty to protect the holders of those rights against deprivation (and these duties can be seen as universal); third, the duty to aid persons to obtain the rights of which they are deprived; this one is less universal simply because the conditions for fulfilling it are not always met. But this does not mean that social and economic rights are not human rights—only that (as the covenant concerning them indicates) the duty of governments is to go as far as it can toward the goal of full achievement, instead of being an immediate obligation as in the case of the covenant on civil and political rights: "that language indicates that fulfillment of economic and social needs may be both an immediate ideal and ultimate right."[11]

This debate is very often presented in terms of value-relativism; such an argument is being made, both in the West and in the Third World. Many spokesmen for Third World countries complain about the Western stress on political and civil liberties; the West, as they see it, tries to impose its own ethnocentric notions on the underdeveloped countries, and makes absolutely impossible demands on countries which are still below minimal subsistence conditions. To require of states which are struggling with misery and chaos the full protection of civil and political rights is resented as a form of cultural imperialism. Interestingly enough, the same argument is sometimes made in the West by people like George Kennan who ask why we should demand of these people that they have the same high standards that we do; they simply are not up to it.

The reality is somewhat different. The Third World complaints conceal a great deal of apologia for evil practices which are being rationalized as inseparable from a low level of economic development without any evidence to prove that this is true. There is no clear correlation between economic development and political rights; the argument that one cannot promote personal and political rights as long as one has not reached a certain level of development is simply not provable, and is oversimplified. A look at the world reveals that the achievement of a more advanced level does not *ipso facto* lead to the granting of political and civil rights in states where these rights have been denied (cf. South Korea); it also reveals that the denial of these rights often leads to the kind of economic development in which many of the rights listed in the covenant on economic, social, and cultural rights are suppressed (cf. Brazil). "Economic development at the price of political oppression has not helped the majority in most countries."[12] Kennan's argument conceals not so much bad conscience as a form of paternalism—manifest when, in a recent book, he asks why Africans have not done in Africa what was done by his Scandinavian ancestors who turned Wisconsin into a blooming state.[13] On the other hand, the Western argument about the superiority of political and civil rights is often simply a rather round about way of defending the market system. The fact is that there is a growing movement to support *both* kinds of rights; this is one of the proofs of this incipient cosmopolitanism I was referring to. Certain forms of behavior, whether they are political and civil or economic and social, are deemed unacceptable anywhere, and the cultural differences which certainly exist do not justify so sharp a split. This is perfectly confirmed by the legal and factual evidence available. Even in countries like the Soviet Union and China, there has been a growing demand on the parts of certain groups for political and civil liberties—just as there had been a demand for economic and social rights in the capitalist countries of the West earlier.

This does not mean that there is nothing at all to the division between the two kinds of rights. But the real distinction does not stem from cultural differences (these are rationalizations or escapes); it is about the role of the state. Even though all human rights require the state to do certain things—that is, to act and not just to omit acting—this notion in itself is rather ambiguous, because many of the rights (particularly the political and civil ones) require the state to do things which will *limit* its powers, whereas many of the other rights, and particularly the economic and social ones, actually build up the state. It is true that the right to fair justice requires that the state provide an independent judiciary and adequate procedures, but the things which the state must thus do are actions for self-limitation and self-denial. The same could be said about maintaining a free press or a disciplined police. However, economic and social rights can only be assured if the state supplies certain kinds of services and benefits for the citizens. There is therefore, in fact, a potential conflict with the personal and political ones, for the emancipation of the individual from traditional social and political constraints has been, as Tocqueville recognized, inseparable from the growth of the modern state, the development of its bureaucracy, the expansion of its scope, justified by the state's mission of providing the citizens with the means to move from poverty to prosperity, from low horizons to happiness. This build-up of the state, in turn, threatens "the individuals' ability to behave as autonomous subjects,"[14] deprives them of meaningful, that is effective, political participation, and affects the independence of groups or the chances of cultural diversity within the state. Thus the problem with the economic and social rights is that they may help the state grow so large as to threaten the political and civil ones. And the problem with the political and civil ones is that they are indeed very often quite indifferent to economic and social reality. As usual, in practice one must try to find some accommodation.

The issue of value-relativism in the field of human rights is of course not limited to the debate between champions of these two kinds of rights. There are cultural differences, most graphically expressed in different notions and methods of punishment upheld by different societies (Americans are frequently appalled at Islamic standards and customs). But "in making allowances for cultural and national differences, one must beware of the danger of sliding into a vulgar relativism, which maintains that the practices of a society can only be evaluated within the terms of its own culture—that no external criterion of judgment can be brought to bear upon them." Not only does this view "erode the moral basis of transnational efforts to promote human dignity," but it conveniently obliterates the fact that most cultural

traditions, albeit in different ways, converge on the same
principles: there are "criteria derivable from all major
ethical systems and acknowledged in many national constitutions." What is true is, first, that this general consensus conceals vast violations; but there is an equally vast
difference between recognizing cultural differences, and
accepting violations "clearly destructive of human dignity, wherever they occur."[15] Secondly, there are disagreements about priorities and about the specific, local
meaning of a given practice. But this only reminds us,
once more, of the danger of moralizing in the abstract,
of the need to look at context and consequence, of the
need to compare the costs of the practice and the chances
and costs of alternatives. Prudence and abdication are
not alike.

The last question about human rights concerns
their status. One has to distinguish between their legal
and their moral status; and here one is again in the realm
of ambiguities. Legally, there is by now a rather impressive network of international documents; they have
served, for instance, as the basis for President Carter's
policy. The main elements are the two United Nations
covenants, which are treaties, the American Convention
on Human Rights, which came into force in 1978, and the
European Convention, which goes back to 1950. However, if one looks closely at these documents, neatness
disappears. Some of them have rather dubious legal
status. About the most sweeping, the Universal Declaration of Human Rights, there is still disagreement as to
whether it is merely a solemn statement of good intentions or whether it has already become customary law.
This is even more true of the Helsinki declaration of 1975
which does recognize human rights in its Principle VII
and in the long and detailed section of its Final Act that
deals with cooperation in humanitarian and other fields.
It is a declaration, not a treaty. In addition, some of the

statements in these legal or quasi-legal documents are perfectly contradictory. The Helsinki agreement proclaims that the participating states will refrain from any interventions, "direct or indirect, individual or collective, in the internal or external affairs falling within the domestic jurisdiction of another participating state." Furthermore, the legal texts are not universally valid: the United States never ratified the two UN covenants, nor the UN convention on genocide. Finally, most of those documents, even when they are treaties, when they have been ratified and have entered into force, are extraordinarily deficient with respect to enforcement procedures. For the covenants, there is a fairly weak procedure of reporting by governments; the covenant on civil and political rights also set up a complaint procedure by individuals which has not been accepted by many states, which must meet a formidable number of requirements to be admissible, and which leads to very little even when admitted. The Inter-American Commission on Human Rights can investigate and report but that is all. The only effective legal mechanism—that of a commission and a court to which individuals can appeal under certain conditions—is the one which exists in Western Europe, which is of course the area that needs it least.[16] Thus if one looks at the legal status, one is obliged to conclude that human rights are of a transitory nature. They are no longer clearly within the domestic jurisdiction of states, but their universal protection is not quite, it seems, a part of the effective international law even by comparison with the rest of international law.

Examining the moral status of human rights leads to a familiar conflict. If we consider human rights to be a domain of moral obligation pure and simple, then we have very extensive duties indeed. As one author puts it, no state can excuse itself by saying, for instance, "We have to continue giving economic or military aid to a swinish state because if we don't give that aid somebody else will." In fact, we would have a duty to twist the arms of those who would step in and give to such a state alternative economic and military aid—unless it could be demonstrated that such pressure on our part would be ineffective or endanger the rights of Americans. A mere *risk* of ineffectiveness would not be enough.[17] There is a second duty, if you think that this is a realm of categorical imperatives: the duty, as Tom Farer puts it (see n. 12), of reasonable consistency. Countries which are alike should be treated alike. We must have clear standards, because inconsistency, resulting from the introduction of nonhuman rights considerations into our treatment of other states, "shreds the moral fiber of the principles a state has proclaimed,"[18] and provides splendid opportunities for self-righteousness in the target countries.

However, if one places the problem of human rights in the realm of real international relations, things are much more difficult. The first question is: Can one really give equal importance to all these rights? Think of former Secretary of State Vance's celebrated Law Day speech of 1977, in which he enumerated all the human rights to which we are committed: it is a formidable list. Can one in practice demand of states that they meet standards which even the United States does not fully reach? (I am alluding to health care, mentioned by Mr. Vance.) Once one starts saying that it is not possible to give equal importance to all, there is no agreement among authors on which ones are *the* basic rights. Divergencies among moral theories, disagreements about foundations have their effects here. Farer (a strong defender of economic and social rights) would make of the individual's rights to physical security the categorical imperative. Jorge Dominguez puts on the top of his list "a people's right to life and health,"[19] which cuts across the great divide and includes both the right to be free of torture, arbitrary execution, and political massacre, and freedom from famine and epidemics.

A second question is far more devastating. Even if one could agree on which of those rights should be promoted first, what about the trade-offs? In other words, can one make of human rights the priority of priorities, as if foreign policy were nothing but the execution by a state of its legal and moral obligations (which would be a very novel notion indeed)? If one looks at the intimidating list of trade-offs presented by Ernst B. Haas,[20] one realizes that it is not simply a choice between the selfless goal of promoting human rights abroad, and the selfish goal of selling arms to or buying strategic commodities from a repressive regime. It can be a choice between attempting to enhance these rights now—at the risk of increasing violence, social disruption, or international tension—and preserving a situation or an evolution that might lead to smoother progress for them later. In other words, human rights are neither the only possible goal of a foreign policy, nor even the only possible moral goal of a non-Machiavellian foreign policy.

FOR AND AGAINST A HUMAN RIGHTS POLICY

Why should there be a human rights policy nevertheless? There are three kinds of arguments. The first are derived from legal obligations. The issue is admirably joined in the Inter-American Commission on Human Rights' report on Argentina. It recognizes that, given the government's obligation to maintain public order and repress acts of violence, the existence of widespread antigovernment terrorism justifies temporary restrictions on human rights, in the case of "extremely serious circumstances." "However it is equally clear that certain fundamental rights can never be suspended, as is the case, among others, of the right to life, the right to personal safety, or the right of due process"; "each government that confronts a subversive threat must choose, on the one hand, the path of respect for the rule of law, or, on the other hand, the descent into state terrorism."[21] These are strong arguments; but they say nothing about the intensity with which outsiders should go about insuring the protection of these rights, and they say nothing about the means. They simply say that state authorities have violated fundamental legal obligations.

The second argument is moral. If one believes that human beings are moral beings, endowed with a conscience, and entitled to live in conditions that allow them to strive for the "good life"; if one believes that society ought to be organized in such a way as to provide all members with the opportunities for personal and moral fulfillment; if one considers that the state's role is to protect such a society where it exists, and to help remove the social obstacles to individual fulfillment where they prevail; if one is convinced that the deep cultural, social, and political differences that underlie mankind's division into nations, peoples, religions, language groups, etc., and above all the borders that separate states, while ensuring the diversity of the ways in which fulfillment can be sought and the difficulty of establishing or enforcing common standards, nevertheless do not deprive any person or group of the rights that derive from their nature as living, feeling, and thinking beings; if one asserts that the fundamental conditions without which fulfillment is not possible constitute the subject matter of human rights, that is of the "just entitlements" mentioned above, then it becomes impossible to pretend that these rights are merely issues of domestic jurisdiction, an affair between the state and its citizens. For this is tantamount to making absolutes of states and borders—a position that either eliminates moral considerations from international affairs, or relegates them to the relations among states, and thus turns states into quasi-persons, even though their legal as well as their moral standing derives fundamentally from the consent of the citizens. To be sure, as we saw in the previous chapter, only the principle of self-determination, not the principle of constitutional, democratic government, is constitutive of the present international order; foreign states are not entitled to intervene by force in order to create or restore internal legitimacy in a given country. But the network of legal obligations mentioned above is both the consequence of the moral conception I have outlined, and the basis for legitimate international concern. This concern extends to denials of a people's right to self-determination as well as to denials of a variety of individual and group rights which are essential components of internal legitimacy.

The third set of arguments, more political (and therefore those with which a political scientist is more at ease), are arguments from world order concerns. In the world as it is, there are increasing threats to human rights because governments have increasingly large means of repression at their disposal, because there is an increasing disproportion between physical and economic resources on the one hand and population on the other, and because the scene is absolutely filled with situations of economic, social, and political instability. "There is nothing new about man's inhumanity to man ... What is new is the known scale of violations"[22]—and what is clear is the risk of a vicious circle of repression and violence. Therefore if our purpose, as I suggested it should be, is an international system of moderate relations, we must remember the connection between the way in which governments treat their own people and the way in which they behave outside. This is one of the clearest lessons of recent history, and in particular of the thirties, when Western democracies, including the U.S., were trying very hard to convince themself that what Hitler was doing with his own people, and especially with the Jews in Germany, really did not mean that he would be equally ill behaved outside. Moreover, when there are widespread domestic conditions of misery and tyranny, the level of international conflict risks becoming extremely high—first of all because those conditions always incite external intervention; and secondly because they also incite leaders to try to find external diversions to internal misery or chaos. There is no way of isolating oneself from the effects of gross violations abroad: they breed refugees, exiles, and dissidents who come knocking at our doors—and we must choose between bolting the doors, thus increasing misery and violence outside, and opening them, at some cost to our own well being. Or else these violations will breed revolt against them, and our own enterprises, or our own security interests, will be affected, if the country in turmoil is one with close links to our own. One can argue quite convincingly that it is precisely a nation like the U.S., with its almost magical fondness for "stability" abroad, that has an interest in defending and promoting human rights there; for if in the short run stability and the status quo appear twins, in the long run regimes of repression and misery will become centers of turmoil and opportunities for "destabilization." In the long run, stability requires—for the U.S.—what might be called progressive change. Or else we shall be caught in an infernal cycle between attempts to perpetuate the ugly so as to defend our interests, and violently anti-American explosions.

But once all this has been said, one also has to be extremely clear about the problems and the obstacles— something which has not always been true in the Carter administration. The case against a human rights policy

amounts to saying that it cannot be done well for fundamental reasons, and that therefore the attempt at doing it
at all risks making things worse off than before. So we
might as well give up, or divorce information and evaluation from policy-making.[23] There are, on this side, three
rather powerful arguments, an argument about who
should pursue such a policy, an argument about its purposes, and an argument about its results. The first argument (in which all who have read Niebuhr will recognize
his thoughts, although he died before human rights
policies were on the market, so to speak) is an argument
about arrogance. Who is good enough to wage a battle
for human rights? I feel that "well-ordered crusades
should begin at home."[24] Before one goes chasing violations outside, one ought to take care of one's own domestic problems, of one's own minorities, of one's own im-
migration policies, of one's own treatment of foreigners,
of one's own willingness, or rather very frequent unwill-
ingness, to let refugees come in, of one's own economic
patterns and policies that make the fulfillment of basic
needs abroad more difficult and tie an impoverished
"periphery" to a bloated "center." Moreover, even if some
nations or some people may think that they are good
enough to take up the fight, does anybody really have the
skills for reforming others? It is not only a question of
being good at heart, it is also a question of knowing how
to reshape the institutions and policies of other countries.
We are in a quandary: from abroad, we can neither rely
on the culprits themselves, that is, on the powers that be,
and that are the causes of the trouble, nor put in their
place humane and wise alternatives acceptable to the
people in question, safe from corruption as well as com-
petent.

   The second argument is about purposes. It is not
enough to agree on the need for a human rights policy;
there are four possible goals which are not at all identical.

One goal is quite simply to help victims; this has been dismissed recently by a man who has the rare distinction of having been a teacher both at Syracuse University and at Harvard, and who is now the senior senator of New York, Daniel Patrick Moynihan, as "humanitarian social work."[25] I would not be quite so contemptuous. Helping victims obviously is not bad, when one thinks of Cambodia, or of Soviet Jews, or of the victims of torture in Latin America. But the question it raises is, again, one of possible disproportion between the means and the end. Just to reach the victims may require shaking heavens and earth; can one really afford this? A second goal which had sometimes been mentioned by members of the Carter administration when they were on the defensive (for instance when they gave a seminar at a university), is general consciousness raising. The advantage is that it is much less costly; you do not have to ask yourself whether you actually help the victims. You please yourself (or you douse your doubts) by saying that your aim, by raising general consciousness, is to make some people feel badly about what they do, and to make them fear what will happen to their reputation and ties to you if they keep doing it. The problem is that you never know how long the consciousness will remain raised if you do not do more than consciousness raising.

The third argument, which is that of the distinguished senior senator from New York, (although he is not a paragon of clarity in the matter) is that the policy should advance the national interest. Fine; but this is either tautological or misleading. If a nation pursues a human rights policy, it means that it has decided that the protection of those rights abroad is in its national interest. But there is a big difference between asserting that this is indeed the case—that the best way to enhance the nation's security, prosperity, and values abroad is to promote human rights in the world, on the basis of the arguments outlined above—and deciding that such promotion will be undertaken only in the specific cases when it directly and demonstrably contributes to the power and prestige of the nation in the world. The first interpretation entails precisely the coincidence of interest and morality, or, if you prefer, the lofty and nonselfish view of interest I discussed in the first chapter; the second uses morality as a selective tool of selfish policy. What happens in that case to the universality of morality, or even to the essence of morality? Does one not become, to go back to Kant, a political moralist rather than a moral politician?

The last goal, the most ambitious, also sometimes mentioned by Mr. Moynihan, is to change evil regimes. A noble ambition. But which ones? All of them? How? And if it cannot be all, which ones will one select? There is a fierce debate in the literature about whether we should try only to change totalitarian regimes, which usually means the Russians (one normally forgets about the Chinese in this discussion, now that they are our friends against Moscow), or whether extremely authoritarian regimes are equally evil. Those who read *Commentary*, or Mr. Nixon, or Mr. Kissinger's latest writings, know all the reasons why authoritarians are supposedly better than totalitarians: because the former "provide some human rights" whereas the latter "deny all;"[26] because totalitarians can never become good whereas authoritarians can; or because these happen to be our friends, and the totalitarians are our actual or potential foes. But if one reads Tom Farer, or the reports of the Inter-American Commission on Human Rights which he now heads, one will find very good examples of governments which are "merely" authoritarian but just as unsavory or unimprovable as some totalitarian ones. When it comes to economic and social rights, totalitarian regimes are not always or necessarily worse than authoritarian ones. And while the scope of civil and political repression may be greater in totalitarian states, it is often a matter of degree, not essence. To wait until authoritarian ones reform or collapse is of little help to victims.

The final and most serious argument concerns effectiveness. A human rights policy may be justified in its principle and clearly focused on a goal. But can it be effective, and what happens—to it, to the initiating state, to the international system—if it cannot? It is an argument in three stages. First of all, at a minimum the policy will corrode morality by inconsistency. States normally resort to a case-by-case approach, and in each such instance the problem of trade-offs becomes dominant, for there is an incompatibility between the human rights priority and the competitive dimension of international relations. In other words, we are engaged in battle against an enemy. This is the relationship of major tension. There is one at present—there normally is one in international affairs—and it is "us" vs. "them." We cannot be very choosy when it comes to us. In other words, considerations of cold war prevail when one is dealing with cases like the Shah's Iran, or South Korea, or indeed China or the Philippines or Pakistan or Romania, since they are on our side or count on us to defend them from the other side. Also, there is an incompatibility between a human rights priority and other essential national interests, such as the protection of American business abroad. A recent report of the U.S.-UN Association on Human Rights, which advocates various kinds of public measures, includes dissents signed by several American businessmen who say that one should not interfere with business for purposes of human rights, because if the government denies companies financial support on such grounds, our markets will be taken up by other countries, and indeed the legitimacy of the human rights policy will be undermined since the public will not support it unless its benefits outweigh its penalties for us. Moreover, they argue, unrestricted trade is a vital national objective.[27] Perhaps even more seriously, there is an incompatibility between a human rights priority and other world order issues. You cannot simultaneously blast the Brazilians for violating human rights and ask them to be good enough not to develop nuclear weapons. You cannot condemn the Argentine junta and expect it not only to curtail grain sales to Moscow, but to refrain from developing its own nuclear program and its own armaments. Nonproliferation, North-South relations, the effort to fulfill human needs within countries of the Third World, détente, the curbing of arms sales, the signing of a new law of the seas agreement, the establishment of a new monetary system, all these concerns are just as important as human rights. If one starts denouncing countries whose support one needs in all of those arenas, where will one be? But if one tries to balance off each of these concerns against human rights, what kind of a crazy quilt will one get?

At worst, according to the second stage of the argument, human rights policies will produce a decisive deterioration of international relations, because the essence of the enterprise is conflictive. When a nation asks foreign governments to improve human rights, whether economic or civil and political, it really strikes at the heart of the other country's political legitimacy and at the heart of its economic system. It is also conflictive because of the tension between the universal aspects of human rights standards and the very foundation of international politics since the days of treaties of Westphalia, which is the principle of sovereignty. Moreover, the means of a human rights policy are by essence interventionary; in other words, it is the opposite of what I praised so much in the first chapter, self-restraint. Finally, the character of the means at the service of such an enterprise breeds inevitable corruption: we start with the intention of doing good and end up conducting political warfare, which is exactly what has happened to the theme of human rights as interpreted by the cold war intellectuals of *Commentary*, for instance.

In the last stage of the argument about effects, a human rights policy is deemed just not workable, because the "good" state will find itself in an impossible dilemma. If that state tries to be consistent, it will radically undermine its position in the international conflict, for it will end up not only hitting enemies, some of whom may hit back (like the Soviets), but also hurting its own friends. This is the argument currently made by Mr. Kissinger, and by Mrs. Kirkpatrick. Human rights policies end up replacing mediocre right wing regimes with hostile left wing ones, or a Pahlavi with a Khomeini, and where is the gain? The outcome is not necessarily better in human rights terms and very bad in national interest terms. Or else, on the other horn of the dilemma, human rights will again become part of a more traditional strategy of national interest, and it will become a sinister farce. In this situation there are a number of possibilities. One is incoherence: each decision may make sense in its own way, but the juxtaposition of contradictory decisions will undermine the human rights policy and demoralize its defenders (in her admirable book, Ms. Vogelgesang gives several examples concerning U.S. policy toward El Salvador: two consecutive and contradictory decisions on a loan from the Inter-American Development Bank for the building of a dam, and two simultaneous and contradictory decisions for an AID grant for a health clinic and against a loan by the Inter-American Development Bank for an industrial project).[28] Another possibility is selective warfare against only one group of delinquent states but not another. This course will foster cynicism abroad and make other countries believe that human rights are being pursued not for themselves but for their value as a weapon. Human rights might even become a splendid cover for cutting foreign aid altogether to "bad" countries, and we all know that most Third World countries can be denounced for not respecting the whole panoply of human rights. A moral pretext could thus be used for a Pilatean policy that will, inevitably, make the outside scene even grimmer.

A brief look at the record, which is bleak, shows the practical force of the negative case. On the good side, there has been, as Arthur Schlesinger points out,[29] some improvement in local consciousness raising, partly because of America's policy, and partly because of the development of a transnational network, a kind of human rights lobby across borders. (Amnesty International has played a noble part in this.) Also, there have been some successes at the margins—prisoners liberated from jails or camps, especially in areas like South America where one could say that a floor had existed before, where some traditions of human rights had developed but where there had been a departure from them. Much less progress has occurred in areas which had never even reached that floor—including much of Central America and Southeast Asia.

On the bad side, the record of the United Nations is, not surprisingly, disappointing. The process that leads individual complaints to the Human Rights Commission remains a slow obstacle course, in which papers get pushed from one body to another. If one turns to the main organs of the UN and looks at whom they have condemned over the years, one finds that, for reasons which are perfectly explainable in power terms, they have excommunicated repeatedly, and heavily, South Africa, (which deserves it, but which clearly also does not have many friends), and they have condemned several times Israel (which does not have many friends); otherwise, and except in the case of Pinochet's Chile, they have been prudent—particularly about the totalitarian countries. This does not mean that they have not denounced the Soviet invasion of Hungary, or passed a resolution about Afghanistan, but I am referring specifically to human rights. The record can sometimes be a little bit better in regional agencies, but not very much. The Organization of African Unity had been extraordinarily reluctant to say anything about Idi Amin, until Mr. Amin was toppled and there was a great deal of uneasiness about the way in which he was toppled, because there clearly existed a conflict between the legitimacy of humanitarian intervention and the principle of sacredness of borders.

Another bad thing is the extraordinary lack of public support for a human rights policy outside of the United States. No other government has really picked it up; even if the former British minister of foreign affairs, David Owen, has written a book called *Human Rights,* Her Majesty's government has not distinguished itself in this area either under Mr. Callaghan or under Mrs. Thatcher. The United States' record itself is internally troubled and externally mixed. Internally, there has been a constant battle of priorities within the Executive, between those who thought that other concerns were more important, and the well-meaning people isolated in the ghetto of the Human Rights Bureau at the State Department. There also has been a battle of zeal between the Executive and Congress, with Congress, until 1979, pushing very hard and the Executive trying to slow it down and to preserve a broad margin of discretion.[30] The external record has been spotty—partly because of external realities, partly because of domestic contradictions. There have been some bright spots, as in the Dominican Republic. There have been some retreats after splashy beginnings, with respect, for instance, to the Soviet Union and to Brazil. There have been some extraordinarily glaring omissions—Iran, Saudi Arabia, Romania, China, South Korea. Sometimes attempts at reconciling conflicting concerns have turned out to be counterproductive, as in the way in which the United States handled Nicaragua during the anti-Somoza revolution (trying to delay or dilute the Sandinista victory), and currently in El Salvador. The methods chosen, such as country-specific sanctions often imposed by Congress, also have been either counterproductive (as in Ethiopia) or ineffectual (as in several Latin American instances). And there has been an appearance of double standards—as some critics have put it, America's human rights policy has ended up being primarily a Latin American policy.

WHAT IS TO BE DONE?

This formidable record of obstacles and disappointments should not discourage one. The reasons for a human rights policy—the moral, the legal, and the political ones—remain strong and would have to yield only if it could be proven, on moral grounds, that an effective human rights policy was strictly impossible, and, on political grounds, that its costs necessarily outweigh the potential benefits. The fits and starts, the failures, the confusion we have found so far do not amount to such decisive proof.

Let us begin with some preconditions for improvement. Not very surprisingly they will sound remarkably like what I suggested in the first chapter: Modesty in purpose, generality (if possible) in action, and much more attention to be paid to problems of assessment.

Modesty in purpose: We should neither request, nor even wish for, a crusade for democracy. The trouble with Mr. Moynihan, whose heart is in the right place, is that he wants a crusade for democracy against totalitarian countries. That is not modest. There are not enough democracies to win. The first art of warfare, if it is warfare we engage in, is to know how to split the opposition, and how to make those compromises that prevent defeat and make it possible to move closer to the goal. If one calls any country that one does not like totalitarian, which he does in a ritualistic way, one's chances of winning are absolutely nil. The purpose a human rights policy ought to have should go beyond mere consciousness raising, and beyond humanitarian social work (although this is not so bad). It ought to be respect for certain internationally recognized standards; but it cannot be, all at once, the achievement of everything that Mr. Vance listed in 1977, simply because that does not exist anywhere. It cannot be the whole bag; what it ought to be is a common floor and a movable ceiling—a movable ceiling, because different countries have different cultural traditions, are at different stages of economic and institutional developments, and face different realities. What you can ask of country A, let us say Chile (which was a democracy for a long time), is more than you can ask of country B, which has never had free institutions and whose economy is backward. A common floor ought to be able to put an end to, or at least to impose an armistice in the battle between the political righters and the economic righters. What I would suggest is what has been argued by Jorge Dominguez: the minimum floor ought to entail the main elements of the right to life and health, which means a fight not only against such things as torture and slavery and political imprisonment, but also against famine, epidemics, and infant mortality. These are precisely the minimum rights which are recognized not only by the international agreements and declarations I have mentioned, but also by most of the world's constitutions themselves. In other words, if countries have been hypocritical enough to put them in the constitutions, they might as well be asked to do something about them, even if these documents are like the ideal democratic constitution of the USSR.

To go beyond the common floor too fast is imprudent. It would not be effective, insofar as effectiveness requires an international coalition. In particular, not all countries can be asked as of now to provide themselves with all the political institutions of Western democracies—perfect freedom of press and association, multiparty systems, free elections. It can be asked of countries that had already reached that ceiling and have fallen below it. But it is only if one remembers the distance from the floor to the ceiling that one can avoid the charge of trying to remake the world in the Western (or American) image.

Modesty in purpose is obviously linked to the second prerequisite, which is generality in action. A human rights policy cannot be one country's policy. This simply cannot work. No country has the means for it, even if it is the United States. The United States has a certain influence on some countries—I will come back to this—but even the U.S. cannot do it all by itself. Gresham's law would operate doubly. First, other states would bail out the delinquents singled out by the U.S. (Bryce Wood points out that Latin American countries can turn to many other sources of military aid, or to multilateral or private sources of economic assistance.)[31] Secondly, as long as one country plays the role of moral judge and moral policeman, it will risk the maximum of distortion and hypocrisy—the maximum of internal backlash if it fails, as we already see in the U.S. today, and the maximum of backlash abroad, where as long as it is an American policy it stirs up strong anti-Yankee feelings, which are perfectly understandable. In other words, just as one has to search for a common floor in substance, one has to look for a common denominator among states, even if it is low. This again is a reason for stressing both economic and political rights. For the coalition for human rights should not consist of Western states only—Third World countries would be suspicious, and one would end with justified but fruitless mutual recriminations about double standards (at present, these countries deplore the Western tendency to be more indignant at, say, black African excesses than at South Africa's institutionalized repression, and Western writers denounce the Third World's monomaniacal emphasis on the crimes of imperialism or racism, accompanied by the defense of their own countries' sovereignty that covers a multitude of sins).[32]

Finally, greater attention must be paid to problems of assessment. When discussing human rights abroad, we must remember that information is often poor and unreliable. It is uneven, with respect both to countries and to ills. The meaning of a given right, say to free elections or to a free press, varies a great deal from place to place. We must know not only what exists at a given moment, but the general direction, the rate of change, the trend, which is more important than the moment. And there are formidable problems of comparability, such as with respect to political prisoners for example. A political prisoner means one thing in one country, and a very different one in the Soviet Union. There are also differences in potential among countries, especially insofar as economic and social rights are concerned. Priority in action ought to be given to the strengthening of all public and private, international and regional, monitoring and reporting bodies. Publicity— the most potent weapon at the disposal of the Inter- American Commission, for instance—is not guaranteed to be effective. But it is a precondition for effectiveness, and enough governments have enough reasons to want a good image. In other words, an essential preliminary would be the mobilization and multiplication of such bodies. We need more specialized ones, covering a bigger scope, (especially with respect to economic and social rights), more public discussion and public meetings; in other words, more ritualization (aimed at obtaining for the conclusions and recommendations of these bodies, the kind of endorsement by international and regional organizations which the Inter-American Commission has obtained from the Organization of American States). And we need more resort to nonofficial members (because state representatives discussing human rights are a splendid recipe for hypocrisy), and more resort to private organizations and transnational bodies. This means an act of faith in the long-run permeability even of particularly hard-boiled authoritarian and totalitarian regimes to such reporting, and monitoring; for they do not live completely shut off.

We next come to the question of means and ends. Let us begin with some general principles. The first one, which will again annoy the pure moralists and philosophers, is that we ought not worry too much about inconsistency. There are two inconsistencies worth discussing. One is more apparent than real—the contradiction between the earlier plea for self-restraint, and a policy of human rights which aims at changing the way governments treat citizens. We must make a distinction between what one can normally call interference or meddling, which is practiced by every sovereign state, and which essentially consists of trying to change a foreign regime so as to make it more favorable to one's own political or economic interests, and the kinds of measures I am advocating here and which are essentially aimed at getting governments to observe rules of behavior to which they have committed themselves. It is an essential distinction.

Everything in international politics constitutes interference, by definition, the minute one gets out of Rousseau's marvelous ideal of little states that have no connection with one another. And the greater the intensity of relations, the more interdependence, the more mutual (and normally uneven) interference there is. But there is a classical difference between intervention in somebody's domestic affairs, which is manipulative and self-serving, and this kind of interference, which even if undertaken among states is in a sense aimed at establishing supranational standards.

The other kind of inconsistency concerns the very substance of a human rights policy. Equality consists of treating different things differently, not equally. And inconsistencies are inevitable, for many reasons. States are in different local conditions; they are situated differently on what could be called the geopolitical map of enmities and alignments; policy has to weigh factors other than human rights (and some of these are moral ones, like peace or the provision of aid for basic needs in countries that violate human rights); and one's power and reach are uneven. To ask for consistency would, in practice, consist of saying that since there are some countries whose internal policies we can never affect, for instance the Soviet Union, we should not try to affect any; that is not very satisfactory.

We must therefore resign ourselves to a modicum of inconsistency. But how much? The next two principles should help us find the answer. The second general principle is that the key question ought to be effectiveness. About each decision, choice of target, choice of means, what is this likely to accomplish? ought to be asked. This has a negative implication and a positive one. The negative one is the duty to avoid grandstanding (even if we convince ourselves that playing to the gallery will raise consciousness, it will mainly raise cynicism and despair if no effective moves follow). The positive implication is eclecticism in ends and means. A modest target that is within sight is preferable to a more grandiose, a more precise to a nebulous one, depending on the circumstances. Here as in other areas of applied ethics the best is the enemy of the good, and the good is measured by the possible. There is no need to prefer public means which are inefficient to discreet ones which can be effective; human rights can be improved sometimes by direct onslaught, so to speak, but sometimes by oblique means. What matters is the effect, or the balance between likely good and bad effects, on human rights.

The last general principle is the avoidance of case-by-case decisions. Am I now being inconsistent? No, because case-by-case decisions of the wrong kind will produce the wrong kind of inconsistency. I am arguing for the right kind of inconsistency. The wrong kind is incoherent inconsistency, instead of defensible and purposeful inconsistency. What is all too often called case-by-case consideration is devoid of a sense of direction and of a strategy: not having a clear place on one's general map of operations, the decision becomes a discrete event unlinked to other similar ones. As in other foreign policy matters, what is needed is purposeful strategy with a set of guidelines. These will take into account cultural differences, local circumstances, differences in trends, differences in the potential of different countries, and the inevitable fact that human rights considerations will have to be balanced against or blended with other concerns. But the main idea would be that the balance or blend ought to be such *as not to sacrifice the promotion of human rights altogether.* There may be instances in which their immediate promotion may be ineffective or counterproductive, or would yield in other important policy areas disastrous results far exceeding the dubious benefits of a frontal attack. In such cases, the direct attempts should be abandoned, but the other policy goals ought to be pursued in such a way as to maximize the chances for future progress in human rights. However, we should never assume that it is a choice of either-or. Countries interested in nuclear weapons will pursue that interest, rooted in considerations of prestige or security, whether we pressure them to respect human rights or abandon the attempt out of pusillanimity. Countries whose political regimes and economic systems make the satisfaction of basic human needs impossible, because of corruption in high places or screens of special interest between the state and the poor, will remain in miserable condition, even if we give to the dream of helping them meet these needs through external assistance, priority over the need to end violations of basic rights. In other words, before we give up, postpone, retreat, and make exceptions, we must carefully weigh, rather than assume, probable costs and likely alternatives. The question ought to be: How far can we go in pursuing the protection of human rights before we start compromising other moral goals, or those Machiavellian goals dictated by general competition and specific enmities that are incompressible, or the domestic basis of support for our human rights efforts? Concerns other than human rights may dictate either a less intense pursuit of the cause of human rights, or considerable discrimination and prudence in the choice of the means used in behalf of this cause. But—especially when what is at stake is the common floor—the cause should continue to make a difference in one's policy.

When one does not have clear (albeit flexible) guidelines, one will always end putting human rights last; they will become like a little bit of salt to be added on the plate at the last minute, or rather not at all, for almost every time human rights will yield to a good argument about something else. You cannot push this country too far; its cultural background is too low. You cannot push

that country too far because it has to fight terrorists, and
the only way of dealing with terrorists is by using their
methods. Or, human rights cannot be pushed too far in
another country, let us say the Shah's Iran, because there
is no good alternative there to the regime in power. Or,
we must be careful here, because we might throw that
other country into Moscow's arms. One needs an inte-
grated policy, not a residual one, a set of clear criteria and
goals, even if they cannot be entirely even and consistent.

This brings us to the question of means and to the
question of targets. On means, we must distinguish between those which are at the disposal of governments and
those which are at the disposal of others—in other words,
the rest of us. Governments, first of all, ought to use not
only sanctions (which are often ineffective or counterproductive) but rewards. (Sanctions are particularly
dubious when they are applied unilaterally: the target
can usually turn to other states. But rewards are often
most effective when they are unilateral.)[33] There is a
blackmailing way of using rewards. "If you want something from me, why couldn't you do this or that, with
respect to human rights." Farer proposes, for instance,
that tariff preferences be given to Third World countries
which meet certain conditions with respect to civil and
political liberties, and to what is called the physical quality
of life index (even that has been reduced to indices). The
other form of reward could be called the enhancing
sort—long-term aid for states willing to promote basic
human needs (see Chapter 4).

Secondly, a great deal can be accomplished by
states deciding simply *not* to do certain things, such as
training local armies or police forces in repressive
techniques—there is no need for the United States to
train the Savaks of this world; or intervening on behalf of
governments that repress human rights, or giving them
military aid when they ask for it. Of course, it is true that

they can turn elsewhere, but that is not always a sufficient reason to give in. My refusal to give aid will not be effective in promoting human rights, if others take my place. But my granting that aid will insure both the perpetuation of violations, and my responsibility for it. In such a choice between two forms of dubious effectiveness, or even when one is faced by one's would-be client's threat to turn, not just to one's own friends, but to one's enemies, there is still a case to be made for providing him with what he wants only on condition that he improves his human rights record, and for the symbolic and political virtues of abstention or omission if he refuses or fails to do so. Whether the jilted state turns to one's enemies will depend on its self-interest; and our main adversary knows what we too have learned: clients are easier to hire than to own.[34]

Thirdly, in the case of rights that are clearly treated as universal and fundamental in contemporary international law (such as the right to be free from torture), pending international agreements that would create a universal criminal jurisdiction against violators of such rights (for instance, against torturers), national courts could follow the example of a recent United States Court of Appeals, which allowed a civil suit, in this country, by the family of a victim of a Paraguayan police offical, against this man who had come to the United States as a visitor.[35]

A last question about means at the disposal of states is: When are sanctions actually justified? They are, first of all, in those cases we discussed in the previous chapter in which even the use of force may be deemed legitimate under certain conditions: cases of genocide, mass slavery, gross violations of physical security; the U.S. embargo of trade against Idi Amin was in this category; secondly, in cases in which governments do in fact promote mass misery, or fail to act against it. There are two

arguments against sanctions which challenge their effectiveness except in rare cases such as that of Uganda (a
country dependent on the revenues from the export of
coffee, whose peasants were already exploited as well as
butchered by Idi Amin). One is that such sanctions—for
instance an embargo on trade with South Africa—would
hurt the poor and worsen their condition. However, this
possible but uncertain result has to be weighed against
the likelihood that the absence of outside pressure would
perpetuate existing, massive deprivations of rights, and
against the certainty that the maintenance of normal
links legitimizes the status quo. The other objection
points to the fact that the economic sanctions which
might be justified would often be effective only if they are
taken by international financial institutions, because
most public aid, these days, is multilateral. For the United
States to cut off its small doses of aid to country X is fine
symbolically, but most of the aid comes from what is
known in the jargon as the IFIS, the international financial institutions. Here, there has been a big debate within
the State Department, between the Executive and many
members of Congress, and also between them and Mr.
McNamara, head of the World Bank. Many have said that
it is scandalous to ask international financial agencies to
use human rights criteria, because their job is development. On this issue, I am on the side of Representative
Harkin, who has tried to prevent, through legislation,
multilateral banks from supporting regimes that violate
human rights.[36] Development is not an end in itself; it is
a means to certain ends. Development that reaches the
poor rarely happens in countries that violate basic rights.
Human rights are internationally recognized; to act to
protect them does not mean politicizing the banks—as if
development and the distribution of aid were unpolitical
anyhow. Moreover, violations have economic effects:
when they lead to massive turmoil opportunities for de-

velopment shrink. And, as has been pointed out by Harkin and others, the measures routinely taken by the IFIS, for instance by the International Monetary Fund, have human rights effects anyhow, sometimes rather debateable ones. Whether Harkin's method was the best possible one or not (that is, whether state representatives on the boards of IFIS should be told how to vote by domestic legislation, or whether it is best to leave instructions to their governments, and to agreements among the governments), his goal was justified; and so is Farer's suggestion of denying drawing and stand-by rights in excess of their gold tranche at the IMF to countries found to be engaged in gross violations of human rights.

To justify sanctions does not mean certifying their effectiveness; the history of embargoes and boycotts is not encouraging. Even if one assumes that a sizable coalition of states has been built up, it may not suffice—hence the importance of the means to be used by actors other than states. Except in the realm of military assistance, states are not necessarily the most effective agents. In economic assistance, private enterprises and banks are far more important. The participation of private groups and individuals in a human rights policy is essential in two forms: as a substitute or as a complement. There is, first of all, a role to be played by national and international civic and scientific organizations, especially in those cases when governments have to put considerations other than human rights, like national security, first, or when governments are obliged to use an oblique approach for the sake of effectiveness. In other words, private groups can sometimes be more effective in raising issues and consciousness, and even in achieving results.

Secondly, when moves by states or by public international institutions are not enough, there is a vital complementary role to be played by multinational corporations or private lending agencies. Can one really ask a multinational corporation or a private bank to "factor in" considerations other than profit? Is not business, or money, their one legitimate objective? Should they suffer the costs of a human rights policy—the loss of markets, of contracts, of jobs at home? Won't such sacrifices be in vain anyhow, as the target countries turn to more reliable suppliers? What about the rights and expectations of shareholders? Surely, the manager's first moral obligation is to them, and to his firm. But is it also his last, or is it his only one? The first answer is that businesses have already become used to injecting concerns other than profit into their strategies in domestic affairs, for prudential reasons. For years they have accepted regulations, for instance labor or industrial legislation, which they do not particularly like, because they have been convinced that it is in their long-term interest. One can do the same with respect to external affairs: in the long run, doing business with gross violators of human rights may lead to upheavals which entail far greater losses than the short-term ones invoked by the defenders of a pure business approach. (Think of American banks and firms that did business with the Shah of Iran.) Moreover, groups which are primarily dedicated to profit may believe that, from time to time, there is a morality above profit; this too is something they do acknowledge at home, where a certain moral consensus exists.

Another answer is that private enterprises and banks, more even than states, can use their influence positively rather than resort to sanctions. Thus in South Africa companies do not have to choose only between participating in and profiting from *apartheid,* and disinvesting. They can try to promote employment, housing and health policies that undermine *apartheid.* And, like states, they can be effective simply by *not* doing certain things: some banks are refusing loans to the South African government. Still, the final answer must be that, when all other efforts have failed to be effective, withdrawal—and the losses it may entail—will have to be the last resort: private groups cannot be above internationally recognized rights, business is not above humanity. However—to close the circle—it is clear that withdrawal will be neither possible nor effective unless it is a policy of several major nations, on behalf of basic rights.

We will end with some remarks about targets. A first target—in recent and undoubtedly in coming years is South Africa, whose *apartheid* system entails institutionalized deprivations of human rights for the black majority, and whose recent moves aimed at some improvement of the economic and social conditions amount neither to the end of exploitation nor to the end of extreme political discrimination. Except for the promise of more business, there are few rewards Western governments and private groups can offer to the white South Africans in exchange for reform. On the other hand, a policy of extreme sanctions, advocated by many at the UN, could be either ineffective, if the main trading and business partners of South Africa refuse to join (here, England is more important than the U.S.—and the West generally is too much in need of South African minerals to go along with a total embargo), or dangerous, if it produces a hardening of the regime and further polarization, leading to a race war and to a possible superpower confrontation. And some trade sanctions (such as an oil embargo) could worsen the lot of the black masses even further. An effective policy would consist of gradual pressure by the broadest possible group of states—enough to give the regime strong additional incentives for change before a peaceful solution becomes impossible, but not so tough as to lead to the counterproductive results just mentioned. One part of this policy would be an effort by foreign investors along the lines described in the previous paragraph—an effort which, in the U.S., the government (for instance through the Export/Import Bank) should encourage, but which is most unlikely to succeed by itself (since improvements in the labor field do not affect political rights, although they may contribute to raising demands for such rights).[37]

A second group of possible targets consists of the developing countries in general, in many of which massive violations of rights occur. They are the most sensitive to cultural (or other forms of) imperialism from the "haves." And their charges of neo-colonialism are very often correct. However, if one tries to introduce human rights considerations into North-South bargains, in which, after all, the West has many of the cards, and if this is done by a common front of a large number of nations for a minimum floor, for a mix of civil and economic liberties, and with equal attention paid to violations committed in developed countries, for instance in South Africa, the argument about neo-colonialism becomes much less potent. I will return to this point in the next chapter.

The third group of targets—not the easiest— consists of totalitarian countries. This is the one where overt pressure and grandstanding are often likely to be most counterproductive. Public statements, public demonstrations of support to dissidents can be justified on two counts: consciousness raising, and boosting the morale of brave, harassed people. But there are huge drawbacks: the fate of the victims is likely to get worse, and objectives other than human rights are damaged. This is no reason to remove human rights from the list of goals. But this is the realm where I would put forth the most passionate defense of obliqueness for the sake of effectiveness. One will never succeed in improving human rights in such countries unless there is first communication, contact, interchange with them. And it is in conditions of general peace, or what used to be called détente before the word became unpopular, that the chances for some diminution of repression are best. It is not a sufficient condition, as we know from the repression that followed the Helsinki agreements (at a time which, however, was no longer the high point of détente); but it is a necessary condition. Governments do not have to be ashamed for putting arms control agreements ahead of a direct attack on and public confrontation over the human rights scene in the Soviet Union, *Commentary* notwithstanding. Peace is a human right (I am not against public confrontation and overt sanctions where they have a chance of succeeding; they may well have one, for instance, in the case of South Africa. But with the Soviet Union this would be counterproductive, for all kinds of reasons. The Soviets are proud, and they are deeply suspicious of penetration and interference from abroad. Their accessibility also depends in part on the general political context and atmosphere of Soviet-American relations.) This is, again, a matter of strategy rather than a matter of choosing between absolutes; any move that diminishes the risk of nuclear war, such as an arms control agreement, creates the conditions in which human rights violations can become a primary target of policy; anything that makes war more likely, or defense an obsession, makes human rights more precarious.

Obliqueness, however, does not mean that one has to remain totally passive about what goes on on the other side. This is precisely where private groups and people have a role to play. The best way for them to advance the cause of human rights in the Soviet Union is not to refuse to hold meetings in Moscow or to have contacts with Soviet organizations. Except in extreme circumstances (such as the Olympic boycott after the invasion of Afghanistan) such lofty refusals of contacts may give one a sense of marvelous moral purity at the cost of total inefficiency. This is a great mistake, because it is only if one starts communicating that one has any chance at all; on the other hand, to go to meetings and do what, according to Arthur Schlesinger,[38] the American Historical Association did at one point, which was to take part in a Soviet-American colloquium in Moscow, very carefully to avoid meeting dissidents or raising any kind of issue, and to behave as if they were groups of equally independent scholars, is a dirty way of washing one's hands. The point is to communicate one's protest and to pressure for change, as the World Psychiatric Association and the National Academy of Sciences have done. Moreover, since most of the totalitarian countries, including the Soviet Union and China, want some things from the West, we can play what could be called not explicit linkage, *á la* Jackson amendment, because it backfires, but implicit linkage. "What you want from us we cannot really deliver to you (because of our public opinion or because of our Congress or Parliament) unless *you* do certain kinds of things with respect to human rights."

The last target area is one about which the most heated arguments have taken place. In my opinion, a state which wants to pursue a human rights policy has a special duty of dissociating itself from human rights violations that occur within its own sphere of influence. We may not be able to do very much about Albania, Outer Mongolia, even Romania or China, most probably Russia, but there are things we can accomplish with our own clients. There are things the French could accomplish with some of their own (which does not mean that they should have just gone and lifted Mr. Bokassa in the way in which they did it, after supporting him for years). In terms of gains for human rights each country has a special sphere of responsibility, and that consists precisely of its clients. There are counterarguments, of course. If we start punishing our own allies, "alienating our friends," are we not undermining our position in the world? Is it

not true that they can turn to our own enemy? Or that
after their overthrow, the successor governments are
likely to be worse? These are scare arguments, in most
instances, rather than valid ones. To be sure, we want
things from them; but if they grant them—bases, minerals, listening posts, etc.—it is because they deem it in their
own interest and because of what we grant them in exchange. This should allow us to subordinate our concessions to progress on human rights on their part, instead
of allowing them to force us, more or less reluctantly, to
give up such demands. If one starts with the assumption
that once somebody is your client there is absolutely
nothing you can ask of him, you will always end up being
victimized by your dependents. In most cases, their current regimes have nowhere else to go; if they go somewhere else, and their new protector is our friend anyhow,
there is nothing lost. And it is the postponement of reform, the persistence in repression, which prepare the
excesses or horrors of the successor regimes. Our policy
should aim at using our influence for human rights
purposes—at blending security concerns and human
rights considerations so as to enhance both, instead of
sacrificing the latter to the former; and if the attempt
fails, we should deliberately, if gradually, dissociate ourselves from the violator. There is, for once, a quite extraordinary coincidence between morality and self-
interest, because in instance after instance—Iran being
the most spectacular—one can show that it is not at all in
America's interest to support blindly unjust, corrupt, and
repressive regimes. These are precisely the weakest spots
in the competitive dimension of international politics.
These are precisely the factors of instability, subversion,
and revolution. Should our clients collapse from within,
while this may not at all improve the human rights situation in these countries, it surely undermines our position
in world affairs for more than attempts at producing

timely reform. And if the client is so fragile that reform could only hasten collapse, it is a good reason for timely dissociation. We may face similar disasters in South Korea, in the Philippines, in Saudi Arabia, and even in Egypt.

In conclusion, let us remember that the promotion of human rights can be indirect as well as direct. Having a human rights policy means not only having a Bureau of Human Rights which aims at establishing among nations respect for a certain code, but above all weighing the human rights effects of *all* one's own policies. In that sense, even if Mr. Kissinger does not like it, the analysis by William Shawcross,[39] and many other people, of the human rights consequences of America's involvement in the Vietnam war is exemplary. It is not to be dismissed simply by the argument that the other side is not any nicer and has committed gruesome violations on a colossal scale. This is true, but since we were unable to win except at a cost incommensurate with the stakes and even more prohibitive in human rights terms, the result of our action has been that the people of Indochina have suffered both the evils inflicted by the other side, and those inflicted by us—and, in the case of Cambodia, those created by our own war actions, the crimes of the Khmer Rouge, and finally those of the Vietnamese.

The next remark, which is discouraging, is that human rights violations are essentially a symptom, and that is why the subject is so difficult. Violations of human rights are the expression of deep structural problems; they are inherent in certain kinds of political regimes and in certain kinds of economic systems in many parts of the world (Latin America, for instance). Therefore, to deal with human rights is to deal with epiphenomena; and yet, given what these violations reveal and given their reasons, this is sufficiently inflammatory to poison the international atmosphere all by itself. If you deal with human rights in the Soviet Union, you don't address yourself to the fundamental problem, which is the nature of the Soviet regime; the same can be said about Brazil or Argentina. However, it is enough of an irritant to make interstate relations difficult. Alas, there is at present no way in which one can deal with those structural problems head on from the outside. We do not have the means for it, we do not have the knowledge, or we do not have the will. Therefore, a human rights policy is a kind of first timid step, *faute de mieux*—an oblique way to handle political change as an international issue.

Finally, when all of this has been said, and after one has tried to define what a policy might be, one sees that there is no way out of the fundamental dilemma. We remain caught between two opposite verities. One is contained in a statement by Professor Richard Falk.[40] He writes that the present system of nation-states has such a high degree of tolerance for violations of human rights, that these rights could be protected only if a new system of world order, not based on the nation-state, were established. The question which this raises, of course, is how Mr. Falk is going to do that? The opposite verity is in a statement by Mr. Kissinger, that in the present system of states the best one can do for human rights is to establish moderate interstate relations, not ask questions about the domestic performance of states, but simply look at how they behave outside their borders. The question which that statement raises is: How are they going to behave outside if their domestic performance is miserable? How are interstate relations going to be stable if intrastate affairs are in turmoil? One is caught in a vicious circle. The aim of a human rights policy is to establish a moderate, livable world order, and yet the precondition for success, for the effectiveness of a human rights policy is that the world already be moderate, that there not be so sharp a distinction between the good and the bad guys, between "us" and "them," as to oblige us to give priority to the security contest, and that there not be too many states or governments depending for their very life on violations of human rights. Given this vicious circle, one should go back to Kant's ideal of the moral politician; the duty of the moral politician is to turn the evil circle gradually into an ascending spiral. One may want to move progressively toward Falk's idea but not take his remark as a counsel of despair about the present. He may be right that only in a different system altogether will human rights be respected, but if you take this too seriously it becomes a splendid argument for doing nothing until we have a nice kind of world government. And one can accept the truth in Kissinger's notion, which is that human rights cannot be the sole objective of policy, yet not take this as a complacent reason for abdicating altogether. But anybody who believes that there is a simple road to progress in these areas has my sympathy.

~~ 4 ~~

Problems of Distributive Justice

INTERNATIONAL INJUSTICE

*T*HE ISSUE OF JUSTICE in international relations is broader than that of distributive justice, which deals with "the proper distribution of the benefits and burdens of social cooperation"[1] and particularly with the proper distribution of economic resources;[2] but the problems of international distributive justice are by far the most troublesome.

Of course, we find again all that we have seen before—the usual incompatibilities between ethical action and the nature of international politics, or the collision between man as a citizen and man as a human being, national and cosmopolitan morality if you like. In addition, we meet here a number of special difficulties. The first one is that, unlike the topic of human rights, the topic of distributive justice really goes to the essence of politics. Human rights may be at the root of all social arrangements, but the politics of human rights is essentially a way of dealing with the surface of the problems caused by political regimes and economic systems, with symptoms rather than with causes. When we examine the problems of distributive justice, we reach the two fundamental questions of politics: Who commands? and Who benefits? It is here that one really gets to the nature of political regimes and economic systems, to the fundamental political causes of injustice. There is a second

141

difficulty; it is over questions of distributive justice that
the conflict of value systems is most acute. In the previous
chapters we found those clashes of values when we
looked at possible solutions to the problems. Here, the
value prejudices or predispositions affect not only the
choice of solutions, but the view one has of the nature of
the problem. When we dealt with human rights, we saw
that there was a dispute between those who thought that
political rights should come first and those who thought
that economic and social ones should come first. But it
was mainly a debate about priorities. When we deal with
the problems of distributive justice, we confront not just a
debate on priorities, but fundamental disagreements
about what constitutes justice or injustice.

The third reason why it is so formidable a subject
is that the difficulties of assessment are even deeper here.
Whenever one tries to define a course of action or interpret what is happening, one is in the middle of the
deepest ambiguity and uncertainty, not only because
one's assessment is colored by the ideological blinders
that one wears, but also for a host of other reasons. There
is a bewildering predominance of what sociologists call
perverse effects; measures advocated as being just are
often likely to have just the opposite effect, or a very
different one from the one intended. Furthermore, the
world is anything but homogeneous. The same course
has different effects in different countries. Countries
following different paths reach comparable results,
countries following the same road end in different
places. One could almost state as a proposition that in this
realm all generalizations are ideological, or least stand on
weak empirical foundations. Finally, our understanding
of social and economic problems remains limited, which
explains the sudden shifts in fashion that have marked
the whole field of economic development.[3] So, there is a
fundamental uncertainty about the best way of remedy-

ing the disease, an uncertainty due not only to value clashes about the nature of the disease, but also to the fact that even within the same ideological camp, one man's remedy is another man's poison. We find here the interaction of embattled systems of ethics, intractable political realities, and extraordinary scientific ignorance.

Not being an economist, I am at a double disadvantage in dealing with what is at the very foundation of economics as a social science—the distribution of scarce resources. First, my discussion is doomed to being nontechnical—a blessing perhaps for some readers, but at the risk of superficiality and naïveté. Secondly, insofar as I have extensively turned to economists for enlightenment, with a political scientist's *préjugé favorable* toward the scientific character of the discipline of economics (by contrast with politics), I have found not only—and not unexpectedly—that the issues of distributive justice, while rooted in economic processes, are so deeply tied to the nature of political and social systems as to be ultimately political issues which require political judgment, but also that they elicit from the economists themselves a chaos of propositions. It is as if anything could be said, and the contrary of anything; and everyone tends to produce evidence without taking into account the opposite evidence adduced by somebody else.

It is therefore not astonishing that philosophers who have looked at ethical issues in political affairs have either ignored the issue of distributive justice in international relations completely (as did John Rawls in his brief considerations on them in his *Theory of Justice*), or else, in the case of those who have criticized Rawls for this, often over-simplified the issues outrageously and remained at a level of abstraction which is really of little use. For it is not enough to state what our duties are. Moral politics is an art of execution; principles unaccompanied by practical means or by an awareness of possible trade-offs remind one of Péguy's famous comment about Kant—his hands were pure, but he had no hands.

I will begin in familiar fashion, by discussing the nature of the problem, and then look at what can be done. In considering the nature of the problem, one ought to ask two questions: What constitutes international injustice, and what are our obligations?

There are two versions of what constitutes international injustice. It is a debate about whether the distributive injustice we are worried about concerns states or concerns peoples. The first version could be called classical. It asserts that the problem lies in the inequality of states. The supporters of this view spin out a whole series of contradictions. The first one is the contradiction between the formal and well-known principle of sovereignty, which belongs to all states, and the absence of what one legal philosopher, Julius Stone, in a slightly convoluted way calls the absence of "equality in the quantum of rights . . . conferred"[4] to states by international law. There is, in other words, a contrast between the fact that all states are supposed to be sovereign, and the fact that the rights which are at the disposal of some states are inferior to those at the disposal of others. This is at the root of the demand which many of the states, and in particular the new ones, have been making for the last twenty or thirty years, for changes in international law— for instance, for the abolition of uneven treaties, or for a change in the law which used to govern expropriations (I am thinking of the 1974 UN Charter on the Economic Rights and Duties of States which grants them "full permanent sovereignty" over all their wealth, natural resources and economic activities). Secondly, there is another contradiction between even the notion of an equal quantum of rights, were it granted, and the material inequality which empties equality of rights of any meaning. It is argued that states require not just equal rights but equal possibilities of development. The famous demands for a new international economic order which have been made by the countries of the Third World for the last years include many which relate to equal chances of development—for instance, those which concern the international exploitation of ocean seabeds (instead of a laissez faire system that would favor the technologically advanced nations), or the terms of trade, or commodity agreements, or the flows of aid, or the reform of the monetary system, or debt relief, or technology transfers. Finally, in this view there is also a contradiction between even a formal egalitarian system of rights and opportunities, were it established, and a highly concentrated system of power. If all uneven treaties were abolished, if all states had exactly the same rights, and even if they were somehow provided with equal possibilities of development, this would still be a world in which power and decisions about international regimes are heavily concentrated in the hands of a few; this is at the root of the demand for power-sharing in international institutions, or of the claim that the poorer states have the right to exercise collectively whatever power they have to change the rules of the game, since those rules are stacked against them—for instance by forming cartels such as OPEC.

Where does this view originate? The people who present it are mostly representatives of the governments of underdeveloped countries, and their case is accepted, at least rhetorically, by several Western governments (the Scandinavian ones in particular). What is the significance of this view? In one sense, as Robert W. Tucker says in his argumentative and incisive book, *The Inequality of Nations*,[5]—a fine critique that leads nowhere—it looks like a demand for a radical redistribution of power and wealth in the international system; but on the other hand it is a rather conservative view of what constitutes international injustice, defined as injustice to the less privileged states, whereas the well-being of individuals is seen as a concern not for outsiders, but only for the state to which the citizens belong. International injustice is a matter of relations between states, like traditional international law. Internal injustice is a domestic matter for each government. There is an assumption here: if only there were a more equal distribution of power and wealth among states, somehow the lot of individuals in the poorer states would improve. This is, of course, no more than an assumption: "greater equality among states may facilitate the promotion of domestic equalities; the former may be a necessary condition, but it is far from sufficient."[6] But it explains (and the fact that this view is largely offered by representatives of Third World governments is highly relevant) why these governments and some of the spokesmen for Third World states are extremely resistant to the idea that the richer states might make their aid conditional on performance criteria to be met by the recipient countries, if those performance criteria should concern the treatment of individuals. As soon as spokesmen of or writers in the developed countries ask "What are you doing with all this aid? Are you not perhaps making inequality even worse, or confirming it?", the answer is, "We are sovereign states; it is sovereignty we are talking about; we want equal rights and power, and for you to look at what we do to our citizens is a violation of our sovereignty."

Not so paradoxically, Third World statesmen have not endorsed the idea—adopted by the U.S. Congress—that aid should be directed at basic human needs (defined by the donor), or the suggestion—made by the International Labor Organization—of basic social norms to improve the condition of low wage workers in developing countries: many of these countries, eager to industrialize, rely on their comparative advantage in labor costs to reach this goal,[7] and they fear that a "basic human needs" strategy would condemn "them to the status of permanent welfare clients, with no prospect for developing to high consumption levels."[8] So this first view, while it looks like a radical demand for change, really amounts to a reinforcement of the state system, as Tucker points out. This is not without a paradox, since after all the "advanced" states, to use that shorthand, are being summoned to assist, to share, and to divest, by developing states which, for their part, say that they have absolute rights of sovereignty over their natural resources. To use Mr. Kennedy's famous description of what Mr. Khrushchev said to him in Vienna, what is ours is ours, and what is yours should be negotiable. There is also a paradox within the paradox: it is representatives of the underdogs, of the hundreds of millions of poor people, who are the most ardent defenders of what Charles Beitz, in his book, calls the "morality of states," the view that in international affairs states, not persons, are the subjects of moral and legal rights and duties.

There is of course another view, not the classical but the radical one, for which international injustice resides not in uneven distribution of power and wealth among states, but in the fate of individuals. When we begin again by looking at the substance of this view, we find that it divides into two different formulations which should not be confused. Both are radical by comparison with the interstate view, but one is more radical than the other; we could call them the moderately radical version and the extremely radical one. The moderately radical view argues that the scandal, international injustice, lies in the poverty of a great part of mankind, of hundreds of millions of people. This is what Richard Fagen calls "equity as non-poverty."[9] In this view, which is shared by Julius Stone, international distributive justice should be concerned with the achievement of minimal rights by individuals. It should go beyond interstate relations, but insofar as individuals are in question it should just be concerned with these minimal rights. This moderately radical formulation essentially says that international justice means providing what in the previous chapter I called basic human rights in the economic and social realm.

On the other hand, the more extreme radical version asserts that the scandal does not just lie in the fact that hundreds of millions of people—40 percent of mankind—are poor. The scandal lies in the causes of that phenomena, not in the phenomenon itself—in the unequal distribution of wealth, not just among states (because the unequal distribution of wealth among states is an abstract matter of statistics, GNP, trade figures, etc.) but among individuals in most states. It is not enough to be concerned with the problem of poverty in the Third World. It is not enough to humanize poverty or to ennoble it, by trying to provide a minimum level of subsistence, so as to raise, so to speak, the floor of poverty to this point. One should, as Tucker puts it, provide course-of-life needs to all: go beyond the mere relief of suffering and try to provide an equal start for all, which is a rather ambitious program.

What is the significance of this view—in either version? Clearly it blurs the distinction between states and individuals, and even deems the distinction illegitimate. It states that problems of distributive justice in international affairs are problems of duties to individuals, and it suggests that the problems of state inequality, which the first view stressed, are either irrelevant or subordinate. What really matters is not that my state has less power or fewer actual rights or chances that yours; it is that the people in my state are poorer than they should be, or more unequal than they should be. Where does this view come from? Here we meet certain surprises.

First of all, the Marxists, whom one would expect some-how to find here, have one foot in this camp and one foot elsewhere. Of course they stress the problem of extreme inequality among individuals in the Third World; how-ever, the individuals are not really their units of concern. They are concerned with classes; and they see in the state—if it has the right class basis—an instrument of progress and change that needs to be protected from outside intrusion and onslaught. The body which stresses the problem of individual inequality or individual pov-erty most is composed above all of Western political and economic writers—philosophers, social scientists, social democrats, and some (but far from all) Third World writers.

One last surprise—the view that justice is a matter of duty to individuals is also held by some Western writers who use the radical moral definition as a splendid way of denying in fact any obligation, of escaping any debt or duty. Thus one of the most brilliant and logical political economists of our day, Richard Cooper, argues that the only moral scandal is the scandal of individual inequality, the only moral obligation is to individuals, because "all of the main lines of ethical thought apply to individuals (or families), not to collectives such as nations."[10] The real horror, thus, is the violation of their basic rights as indi-viduals. However, international relations, alas, only deals with states, and in interstate affairs the only con-siderations are prudential ones, not moral ones (or else "a new set of ethical principles applicable to nations must be developed"). Let us combine these two ideas. The result is complex. On the one hand, there are, on prudential grounds, areas of mutual gain to developed and develop-ing states that should be explored; on the other hand, in interstate dealings, the only resource transfers justified on ethical grounds are those which would ultimately help individuals. What does this really mean? It is a very roundabout way of saying one of three things. It could be a way of saying, "Let us not, on liberal grounds, give Third World states any assistance at all, since many of them are corrupt, all of them object to externally imposed performance criteria, and the money will therefore not go to individuals." Or else it could be a way of saying, as Cooper does, that we should not give them any large or automatic package of assistance, since we cannot control whether it will really help individuals, and since (on prudential grounds) most of the assistance is likely to be given to the better-off developing countries, in exchange for political services, and with no direct relation to poverty. Or else it may be a way of saying: Let us give them only the kind of assistance which is supposed theoretically to reach individuals. We cannot see whether it reaches them or not, because that would violate the states' sovereignty, but there is a theory which assures us that it ordinarily will: it is classical liberalism, it is the "trickle down" theory. But the only "assistance" it justifies is liberal trade. These are, then, three different ways of minimizing the response to the problem, while starting with a very radical formulation. This shows already something we are going to find throughout this chapter: that the diagnosis is often tailored to the desired prescriptions rather than the other way around. And it also shows that the analysis of the nature of international injustice leads into that of our obligations.

OBLIGATIONS

The problem of international injustice could have been described as states vs. people. The question of the nature of our obligation is different. What do we owe whom, and why? There are two debates: one about the scope of our obligation, and one about its foundation. In other words, how wide is it? How deep is it?

Let us start with the debate on scope. What are we, as citizens or as governments of the richer countries, obliged to do? There are three principal positions, a minimalist one, a maximalist one, and one which is in between (and where I find myself, not too surpisingly). The minimalist position consists in saying that we have no duties toward states or people other than our own, that our duties are to our own community only. In other words, it may be a matter of self-interest or prudence or charity to watch over conditions in the rest of the world, but it is not a matter of moral obligation; even if the ultimate scandal is the plight of individuals in three-fourths of the world, there is no duty. Why? First of all, the argument goes, there is no obligation concerning distributive justice toward other states. Justice is among indivduals. Relations between states are not concerned with justice; they are concerned with power and status. To treat the demands of Third World countries as if they were demands relating to justice would be a serious mistake. According to Robert W. Tucker (whose case resembles that of nineteenth-century conservatives opposed to universal suffrage or to welfare legislation), it would lead to two disasters. One is a disjunction between order and power. To grant or devolve power to them, to accept their view that such a transfer is only just would mean that the only states that can create order—that is, the states whose might and wealth give them a stake in the established system—transfer power to states which do not know what order means or are incapable of creating one. Note the equation of order and hierarchy: the diffusion of power is tantamount to anarchy.[11] The other calamity is a disjunction between order and justice. Justice is seen, by the new egalitarianism of Third World states and by the "new sensibility" of Westerners concerned about the plight of individuals in the Third World, as distinct from, indeed opposed to, the existing order of the powerful. This is distressing, both because in international affairs justice presupposes order—without order there is only the injustice of chaos—and because it confuses interstate relations with relations of justice.

Having thus disposed of the notion that we have duties concerning justice toward other states, this brief turns to a second argument: that we have no duties concerning distributive justice toward individuals in other states. There are several reasons for this. First, there is no general community of mankind. Obligations to other people exist only if they are all part of the same community. We may be interdependent with others, but interdependence is a material fact, community is a moral fact. Domestic institutions are real; international institutions have weak roots and power, they are epiphenomena. Secondly, we have domestic obligations of justice because the national community is a special kind of bond from which obligations and social roles are derived. None of this exists in the world at large. Lastly, there is a psychological reason: no person can respond to the full range of human misery.[12] One has to draw the line, and the limit is taking care of one's own.

There is a third argument which covers both obligations (or rather the absence of obligations) to foreign states and to foreign individuals. It is partly a utilitarian one. If we had a duty, we could not discriminate between "good" foreigners and bad ones—between deserving states, and hostile, unstable or inefficient countries, between deserving poor and idle ones waiting for an external dole. The argument is also partly categorical, and addressed to Americans: our central value is liberty, not the abolition of poverty.[13] Clearly, this is a rather shabby case; in political affairs, as we have stated often, morality is never simply a matter of principles, it always entails the weighing of consequences. And the assumption that liberty and justice are mutually exclusive is absurd; liberty may predispose one toward certain ways of coping with injustice, and against certain other remedies. But where there is extensive injustice, basic liberties are impaired. Needless to say, against the minimalist view a maximalist one has developed. It claims that our obligation concerning justice is universal, that despite the existence of separate states and nations we have a duty to all mankind. This view starts with the refutation of the previous arguments. The most recent such attempt is the book of Charles Beitz. First, he says, it is true that international society is imperfect, but this is no excuse: "the ideal cannot be undermined simply by pointing out that it cannot be achieved at present."[14] It could be undermined only if one could prove that "authoritative global institutions" and a sense of global justice could never be attained or would have undesirable results. Secondly, while it is true that we have strong natal sentiments toward our community, we should not confuse natural sentiment with moral obligation. To put it bluntly, our obligation of justice toward the Bantus is exactly the same as our obligation of justice toward our immediate neighbors. Or, as he puts it elsewhere,[15] voluntary obligations (like those which exist in a community) do not always override nonvoluntary ones. Finally, the psychological argument that nobody can cope with all of human misery is countered by the assertion that this is not valid against very broad violations of human rights. There is no possible reason that could justify a violation of the principle that all human beings have the same moral standing.[16]

The result of this view, in the opinion of Beitz and some others, is a plea for a worldwide application of Rawls's principles of domestic justice—exactly the kind of thing Rawls did not do, so that Rawls always gets lectured at by his critics for having stopped at the borders. His assumption (in the few pages he devotes to international affairs) is that states are self-contained units, and therefore very little is necessary in terms of principles of justice governing relations among them. If you do not accept this view, if you believe that our obligations of justice to people are universal, there seems indeed no reason not to apply Rawls's two principles of justice, devised for domestic society, to the whole world, since the states are not self-contained. There seems to be no reason in particular not to apply an international difference principle (an extension of his second principle, which prescribes that social and economic inequalities should be arranged so that they are to the greatest benefit of the least advantaged, and attached to offices and positions open to all under conditions of fair equality of opportunity). In other words, we have a duty of minimizing intrastate inequality, the inequality which exists among people in any state, so as to maximize the position of the globally least advantaged group; a tall order. Beitz applies the same notion to the problem of entitlements to natural resources. Since it is wrong "to suggest that we can only have moral ties to those with whom we share membership in a cooperative scheme," he believes that the parties meeting in the original position would agree on a resource redistribution principle: "each person has an equal *prima facie* claim to a share of the total available resources, but departures . . . could be justified . . . if the resulting inequalities were for the greatest benefit of those least advantaged by the inequality."[17] Another tall order.

　　So tall that there is, necessarily, a third position, which is an intermediary one. It starts by arguing that the maximalist one—the view that we have equal duties to all individuals all over the world—is just not tenable. This can be shown, first of all, on prudential grounds: the Beitz view is thoroughly inapplicable. If his case were right, a donor would have to give, almost automatically, precedence to others, all of the others abroad who are poorer, before using any of his own resources for domestic self-improvement. Before I can spend a penny on the poor in the Appalachians, I have to spend all I can on those who infinitely poorer in Bangladesh. That is not the way politics can work. And as for the recipients, they would have, in effect, to let the donors decide how transfer payments are to be distributed—otherwise the poorest in the recipient state might be left unhelped—and they would have to abandon their sovereignty over natural resources, since Beitz states that nobody has a full right on natural resources at all. Beitz' view, from the viewpoint of prudence, is a complete negation not only, as Tucker puts it, of history, but of the political dimension of politics. Secondly, on ethical grounds, it does not work because Beitz, once more, discards the moral dimension of national politics as well. States may be no more than collections of individuals, and borders may be mere facts. But a moral significance is attached to them (see Chapter 2), and this is precisely what the worldwide extension of the "original position," the turning of what in Rawls's book are representatives of *nations* into denationalized individuals legislating justice for an undifferentiated mankind ignores. Moreover, as has been pointed out,[18] if one applied the Rawlsian principles across borders, it would mean that a state which is domestically just—which meets in its borders the requirements of Rawls's principles—could still be obliged to transfer resources to a poorer state (and perhaps make itself unjust in the process); certainly this would have to be justified on other, stronger grounds, than the mere reference to the two principles of justice. "The problem of deciding 'why' as well as 'what' and 'how much' is difficult enough in a national society; it promises to be impossible in a world where men have different cultures, religions and outlooks even if they have lost their nationality."[19] One is left with the old Kantian notion, that when there is unfeasibility, impossibility, there can be no obligation.

However, and this is why an intermediate position is possible, there is a core of wisdom in the maximalist view. As Beitz says in an article,[20] the existence of domestic community obligations, for instance of strong obligations of justice to fellow Americans, does not obliterate global obligations. (The minimalist view, logically, would deny obligations of justice even toward people who live on one's community's soil yet are not part of it, such as refugees or immigrant workers, except perhaps for providing a minimal level of subsistence.) And, as others have pointed out, one can, after all, positively find a beginning of a sense of duty toward people in other countries, especially in matters such as famine or natural disasters.

A compromise view emerges, which is the following. One can adopt neither the interstate nor the interindividual framework exclusively. First, international justice is a matter both of rights of states and of rights of individuals. Secondly, there are obligations of justice to other states. The claims of those states are not only claims for power and for status. Insofar as they are claims for wealth, they must be considered for the sake of distributive justice. Thirdly, however, one has to keep in mind that states exist only as communities of people; states are not divinities, their rights are rooted in the presumption of fit between them and their people; and this does put a kind of damper on the demands of the Third World governments for absolute sovereignty, for impermeable state rights. We may feel that we have a duty to share some of our wealth with them, but only if that wealth is used toward justice for those communities of people. This also means that all equity claims presented by Third World states are in a sense conditional on their doing something for their people. Fourth, when it comes to the issue of how much we actually owe the Bantus, my position is close to Julius Stone's. International justice by now should *at least* be concerned with the minimal rights of all people, the first formulation of the radical vision. One cannot say that we have already an obligation to full equality for everybody, everywhere for two reasons. One is that there is as of now no way in which we could meet such an obligation. After all, it is not possible, in helping others, to go beyond what can be consented to domestically. You cannot violate your own public opinion in this matter. You should educate it; you should make it less parochial or selfish; but you cannot go so far ahead as to be rejected. The second reason is the possibility of a moral conflict between making subsistence available to all, and starting with the poorest in one's own nation—between the practical consequences of the most radical formulation, which treats mankind as an undifferentiated entity, and those of the view that stresses the moral priority of the nation. Each view stands on strong moral grounds; neither one is acceptable if one insists on excluding consideration of the other. And therefore I end up somewhat inevitably with the philosophically untidy and politically elastic notion, that the scope of our obligation to individuals in other societies varies in time and in space. There was none of it perhaps sixty or fifty years ago (or rather, very few people acknowledged one). There is some now, more widely recognized. If all goes well, and statesmen, writers, and so on, press on, it may grow in the future. Our sense of obligation is of course strongest in our own community, but it also exists within larger groups, communities intermediate between the national one and mankind (let us say, the European community, for West Europeans), and it gets weaker as one goes farther away.

To sum up, our obligation of justice is not just to

our own people; when it comes to obligations to other individuals we are acknowledging obligations of mutual aid to states in order to improve the lot of their people, and particularly of their poorest people, but the scope of these duties is somehow still in an evolving position in time and in space—except, I would say, insofar as there are violations of the most elementary human rights of other individuals.

The second question about what we owe others entails a debate about the foundations of obligation. How deep is the sense of duty that we have toward others in other societies? And what does it stem from? Here there are other difficulties. In the literature on this subject, first we find the argument that we must feel obliged because we are all guilty. Our obligation as citizens of rich states derives from our misbehavior in the past; we owe reparations to the poor states and their people. It is a kind of tribute. This I reject for a number of reasons. Psychologically, I think it is the most counterproductive argument; the only result of trying to inject a sense of collective guilt is the generalization of resentment, not a feeling of obligation. Just think of what has happened in history each time such a guilt clause has been imposed, or think about the history of reparations—what it did to Franco-German relations after 1871, or to Germany's relations with the rest of the world after 1919. Also, historically, this is Pandora's Box. Let us assume that our ancestors have indeed harmed millions of people. How far back in time do you have to go? When did malfeasance begin? Who is supposed to pay? Is it just the descendants of the people who went and exploited them, is it all of us? We are dealing most of the time now with what Karl Deutsch would call "socially mobilized publics," or "democratic publics," even if the regimes are not always democratic. Now, one of the principles of democratic publics is that they do not accept responsibility for the sins of their ancestors. As Tocqueville put it, each generation believes it begins anew. And you will never be able to convince people in this country or in England or in France that the aid which they feel a duty to give, they must provide because their ancestors were brigands and exploiters and murderers. It is not a suitable basis of obligation.

Finally, scientifically, the argument of exploitation is quite unprovable. We cannot prove what would have happened to India or Bangladesh or Pakistan or Africa if colonialism had never occurred. After all, there have been considerable variations there. Some countries which were never ruled by colonial powers did no better than those that were colonized. Some colonized countries did far better than others. Nor do I know how one assesses the evils of colonialism as a yardstick for present duties, because one would have to calculate intangibles. On the one scale, as the defenders of colonialism always do, one puts law and order, and what figure do you give to this? On the other scale one must indeed put the disintegration of existing communities, or the forced mergers of communities which explode later on, or the destruction of native institutions, or the lack of self-respect, or the feeling of being exploited even when it goes far beyond the actual provable economic exploitation. How do you weigh that?

If one says that it is not just a matter of colonialism; that exploitation is the result of what the rich did to the poor, whether the rich took colonies or not, alas, there are enormous disagreements about what constitutes exploitation. It is a fundamentally unscientific and subjective notion. In the case of Latin America, Tony Smith has recently demolished standard arguments about "decapitalization" and "denationalization";[21] and Richard Cooper has argued that the greater profitability of overseas investment is in doubt.[22] But for Johan Galtung, practically any kind of trade, except the barter of simple objects, is a nucleus of imperialism.[23] Again, all attempts at measuring what would be due in restitution have failed, for the best of reasons. What would constitute a good quantitative index? James Caporaso's attempt to use terms of trade as a "ready measure of exploitation"[24] foundered on a variety of empirical and conceptual arguments. How could the sum be converted in current prices? Nor is there any agreement about the effects of exploitation, between those who stress evident possibilities of resistance, and those like Johan Galtung who find it at the root of practically all institutions and forms of conduct.

A second foundation of obligation is suggested by the absolutist argument that like all other moral obligations it comes from our consciences. Here we are in a difficult area too. On one point Richard Cooper is right. Conscience is matter of relations between individuals, or between individuals in families or in voluntary groups. When we talk of obligation to other states, then is this really a matter of conscience? Is it not an obligation that is conditional on their performance, and no longer a categorical imperative (and therefore often resented by the recipients)? Furthermore, it is fairly clear that our sense of moral obligation is far from universal because, within a given country, those who recognize such duties beyond borders are often not even the majority. The people whose consciences are so strong that they feel, as citizens of the rich countries, that they have duties both to the states and to the individuals of the Third World are, as Julius Stone puts it, enclaves, and normally small enclaves, of liberals—I do not say guilt-ridden liberals because I do not like the rhetoric or the clichés of the conservatives and neoconservatives. Even the sense of obligation which exists in those enclaves has limits of scope that we have already discussed. They do not feel a duty to promote full equality at severe costs for the living standards of their own people, and, to go back to an earlier argument, they do not feel a duty to give aid to states that may be aggressive, or totally chaotic, or totally ineffective. As usual in moral politics, pure conscience is not enough.

Do we encounter here what is normally behind obligation in international affairs, as I laid it out in the first chapter, a combination of conscience—at least incipient conscience—and calculation of interest, or moral sense and prudence? There are more difficulties. What kinds of interests are in evidence? The literature offers many arguments about mutual benefits, and they are most important for persuading the publics of advanced countries—pure moral appeals would not suffice. A commission headed by Willy Brandt has just produced one more report on North-South relations, and it lists once more a whole series of possible mutual gains—in commodities, in trade, with respect to multinational corporations and to the international monetary system, etc.[25] These are mutual economic benefits. The mutual political benefit is our joint interest in orderly change. It all sounds very good on paper. However, orderly change is not the goal of all states and is far from certain to happen even if one transfers resources and provides all kinds of assistance. And as for economic interests, there are many important mutual gains, but unfortunately they are often long term. Moreover, those long-term mutual interests exist primarily with the wealthiest of the poor nations, because they are the ones with whom we deal most. It is the least needy with whom we have the most mutual interests. The neediest either we do not need, or else—in those cases where we *do* need their raw materials—they are too weak either to absorb enough of our exports or of our surplus investment capacity, or to be much of a bother. In the short term, aid costs a great deal. In the long run, the huge potential market of the developing nations may serve as an engine of growth for the industrial ones, but in the short run there are all the costs of adapting to the competition from the imports of the manufactured or agricultural products from the developing countries. In the short run, as we can see from looking at the story of OPEC in the last six years, our interests are very often antagonistic. The question raised by the interest argument is: "Can long-term, diffuse mutual interests prevail over short-term, intense national ones?" And the answer which the democratic publics also very often give is: "No, the priorities should be our immediate interest." As it was put in France, the interest of the department of Corrèze should come before the interest of the Zambèze, or the Bretons should come before the Algerians.

There is another kind of interest argument which is not in terms of mutual benefits. It is an uglier one. It is interest derived from fear. We should give them something, because they can do an enormous amount of harm to us. That is the argument made by C. Fred Bergsten.[26] Economically they can harm us greatly by cartelization or by just falling into chaos. And politically they can harm us by refusing to cooperate in the establishment of international regimes, or by promoting nuclear proliferation, or by siding with our chief rival. The trouble with this argument is that it does not work to reenforce a sense of obligation, for all kinds of reasons. First of all, the number of possibly successful cartels is limited. Most products do not lend themselves to cartelization, unlike oil, and many raw materials are produced by the developed nations. Secondly, the greatest risks of economic chaos happen to exist in those countries which are least linked to the wealthy. If Bangladesh or some of the other really poor countries sank into chaos, we could afford to be extraordinarily indifferent. Politically, it is true that even they can do harm, for instance by turning to Moscow or by throwing us out; but they might do that same harm if we aided them economically but without resolving their formidable internal problems (think of Iran, or Egypt). It is not a one-to-one connection. Finally, like guilt, fear—in those cases where it is justified, as in our relations with OPEC or with other Third World states wealthy or advanced enough to foster nuclear proliferation or to spread political chaos—is an extraordinarily bad and shaky psychological foundation for obligation. Moral obligations must come from within (as they do even when we find a calculation of interest behind them). Fear constrains and coerces, it does not oblige. Within a nation, fear can be effective because it is the fear of superior power: the police, the judge. In international affairs, fear is more likely to breed resentment, to provoke reaction and backlash.

Does this mean that there is really no foundation, and that all we have toward the poor is a kind of duty of charity? There is one school of thought which says just this; that is the school of thought represented by *Commentary* and the *Wall Street Journal*. (One name is common to the two: Irving Kristol.) All we owe the poor is charity, because we are good Christians, or good Jews, or out of prudence, but we have no obligation of justice really. Indeed, to say that we have an obligation to the poor is very bad for us and for them, for us because it could lead them into extortion—into reverse imperialism[27]—and for them because they would be self-indulgent, they would sit on their poverty and just wait until we fulfill our obligation. Charity of course is conditional on their behaving like good dependents. In other words, nothing is due to them anymore if, to quote Kristol, "the poor should start Mau-Mauing their benefactors."[28] This is clearly totally insulting to the poor abroad (just like the argument that welfare is not in the interests of the poor at home, since it damages their self-esteem). And it is most unacceptable insofar as basic human rights, such as the right to food, are concerned. Charity denies the structural roots of radical inequalities. And if it cannot be said that it has been as entirely superseded in international affairs as its has been in the domestic realm, there are enough doubts about the legitimacy of the international distribution of resources—whatever the disagreements on causes and remedies—to have blown away the good conscience of simple charity.[29]

Where do we end? With a question mark, which is not the first time, about how deep our sense of obligation is. This is not so surprising. We are dealing with something inconclusive, because it is of an intermediate and complex nature. Our duty is partly to states, partly to individuals. And our state of conscience is somewhere in-between the argument that we owe nothing, except a dole, outside of our community and the argument that we owe the same thing, full justice, to all mankind. So it is not shocking to find that the foundations of obligation are still shaky. It does not mean that we should not work at making them stronger and firmer. And yet, it is a discouraging conclusion, but "I never promised you a rose garden," either in analyzing where we are, or in suggesting how far we can travel on the road we ought to follow. We must never forget that the problem of distributive justice, like that of force, looks fundamentally different in the context of the state and in that of the world. Within the national community, either through the work of political and intellectual leaders, or through the efforts of the state, we usually find a consensus on what constitutes justice—a consensus that can evolve dramatically, as the American New Deal and the post–World War II West European welfare state show. And it is through the state that the common standards of justice get refined and enforced. In the international milieu, there is a cacophony of standards—Marxist ideas of social justice conflict with social-democratic and with laissez faire notions—and the instruments of enforcement are the separate states; which means, unhappily, either that justice becomes a matter of sheer force—carried at the point of a sword—or, when force does not prevail, a matter of fleeting bargains and tests of fear or strength. In the absence of a "world market" of opinion, and of supranational institutions, how could the sense of obligation be anything but flickering?

DIAGNOSES AND PRESCRIPTIONS

What, then, should we do, and what can we do, to strengthen and to carry out this very fragile sense of duty? Here is where we find ideology taking over completely. We shall have to answer in two phases. First of all, since the remedies depend on it, what is the diagnosis— what are the roots of injustice? And secondly, what should we do to promote justice? I assume that we have found *where* injustice is: both in relations between states and in the plight of individuals. We still have to understand where it comes from before we can establish what to do about it. However, when we examine the roots of injustice we find the cacophony almost deafening. There are many different positions; I will discuss, rather briefly, three of them, of which two—the chief antagonists—are familiar enough to allow for the sketchiest of summaries.

The first position is the radical one. The roots of injustice are in the economic system. This charge comes in several different forms. The first puts the blame on the operations of the international economic system. The most impressive presentation can be found in a collection of essays by Keith Griffin, an Oxford economist.[30] He makes an anti-Ricardian argument. International intercourse increases inequality and poverty and leads to the disintegration and dependence of the Third World. All of the asymmetries in international economic intercourse are at the expense of the poor: they depend heavily on international trade in which they have only a very small share; they are very limited in power yet face powerful multinational corporations (which control much of their foreign trade and can therefore limit the earnings these countries can derive from exports).[31] The concentration of technology in the rich countries also operates at the expense of the poor ones: we mobilize their savings and their skills, and we export the wrong kind of technology—capital-intensive technology—to them. All of this has been intensified by the Bretton Woods system— the postwar international monetary regime—and by the postwar international economic system: the payments schemes, the possibility for the rich to protect themselves from competition by the manufactured products of the poor, the voting mechanisms in international financial institutions, all have worked against the developing countries. The distribution of international reserves and of value added in the products traded between rich and poor countries favors the former.[32] The same indictment of the world market economy has been presented by a philosopher, Thomas Nagel (cf. n. 29).

Another version, which is also present in Griffin's book, and of course in many others, traces injustice to the domestic system in most of the poor countries. Economic development in the Third World produces a clash between equity and efficiency. Economic growth increases inequality in income and in other factors. When the income distribution is distorted the market allocates resources unfairly. The obstacles to change are constituted first of all by the nature of modern industrial development—capital intensive where it should be labor intensive—secondly, by the nature of the elites, who have an interest in perpetuating inequality and are the captives of a "catch-up mentality" that distorts development (slanting it toward the import or production of luxury goods);[33] thirdly, by the nature of the state, which depends on those elites; and all of this is cumulative. Poverty produces insufficient growth. Concentration on raw materials or crops for export retards the expansion of food production for the population. Concentration on a few industries for export leaves masses of unemployed. The credit system in the poor countries favors the rich. There is a split in the labor force between skilled labor, working mainly for the advanced and exporting sector, and the rest of the workers; and these countries have no means to create wealth.

In either version, whether one puts the blame on the international market or on the the domestic market, it is the capitalist system which stands indicted. A third version links the other two by focusing on the capitalist mode of production. It is the famous "center-periphery" model developed by a number of Western and non-Western, Marxist, and quasi-Marxist economists and sociologists—André Gunder Frank and Samir Amin,[34] Arghiri Emmanuel and Johan Galtung.[35] In Amin's words, "This model of accumulation at the periphery of the world system begins, under the impetus from the center, with the creation of an export sector in the periphery which will play the determining role in the creation and shaping of the market." What follows is "the essential theory of unequal exchange." The wage rate in the periphery will be as low as possible. And in the periphery, by contrast with the process at the center, capitalism is introduced by outside domination, class alliances are not internal but international, and external relations determine development. In Galtung's words, capitalism is related to more problems, to more fundamental problems, and is more deeply rooted than other evils (such as what he calls "social imperialism").

Next we turn to the opposite view. It is the traditional liberal theory which says that in effect one should have faith in the market. Were the market to operate in optimal conditions, all or almost all would be well. The theory of comparative advantage assures that a mutually beneficially specialization of production would develop between developed and developing nations. Trade, if it is not impeded, will reflect the division of labor, bring gains to each country, and lead to an equalization of factor prices and of incomes across borders. Multinational corporations investing abroad in search of higher profits will increase the income of the poor, diffuse advanced technology, and enhance economic activity in the poorer country. If there is injustice, it results not from the market, but first of all from differences in national endowments, about which one can do little; secondly, from market imperfections, from all the obstacles to the free flow of goods, people and capital; and, finally, from domestic policies either when they throttle the signals which the market gives, and prevent, for instance, wealth from trickling down by premature reforms, or else when they simply neglect the problem of inequality and forget to counteract the temporary contribution of economic growth to inequalities, or even sharpen these: a "vicious circle of poverty" can occur, but adequate measures could prevent its institutionalization.[36] This suggests a separation between the style of development (Fishlow's phrase), and the nature of the capitalist system. Thus we have two completely opposite views of the roots of injustice.

Needless to say, there are others. One of the most interesting intermediate views is the one expounded by Arthur Lewis, in his little book, *The Evolution of the International Economic Order*.[37] He sees the root of poverty and inequality in the domestic system of the poorer countries, but not in the capitalist mode of production. He puts the blame on the absence of an agricultural revolution in Third World countries, including, incidentally, countries which were not colonized; the absence of such revolution foreclosed the possibility of industrialization for them, left them only with trade rather than industry as their engine of growth, and put them thereby at the mercy of the market, in which the terms of trade for tropical goods were bad. "For temperate commodities the market forces set prices that could attract European immigrants, while for tropical commodities they set prices that would sustain indentured Indians."[38] This became cumulative. Industrialization was further hampered by foreign control of import and export trade, and by the domestic elites, often dominated by agricultural interests. One ends up with the dependence of the poor on the rich countries, both for financial reasons (the population explosion leading to urbanization, which requires extensive borrowing from abroad) and for commercial ones (trade remaining the engine of growth, the developing countries depend on their ability to penetrate the markets of the advanced ones).

One of the reasons for mentioning these conflicting diagnoses is that each "explanation" breeds a specific set of remedies. The radical vision leads to an inevitable conclusion. The solution can come only by revolutionary means—a drastic transformation of the social system in the poor countries, leading to an overhaul of the international economic system—for instance, by a massive switch to self-reliance on the part of the poor, and collective severance between the poor and the rich. Advocates of self-reliance range from moderates (such as Haq) to extremists (such as Galtung or Amin); but all stress a turn to mass consumption goods, the maximum use of local technology and exploitation of local resources, especially in agriculture, the reduction or elimination of dependence on foreign aid, and increased cooperation among the developing countries. For many of the authors, only a political revolution can achieve these results. As Fagen sees it, a reformist state relying on private capital and foreign investment for its development does not have a chance. The liberal view, on the contrary, suggests measures to remove market imperfections and to make market signals clearer and more reliable. This may entail a fight against monopolies, and selective delinking—diversifying sources of dependence; it involves neither the collectivization of agriculture nor public control of the means of production. It suggests the opposite from the regulation of the domestic and world economies by governments, from the replacement of the market by bartered agreements, from the systematic distrust of multinationals which the radicals advocate. Lewis' vision leads to a very different imperative: to switch from trade to technology as the engine of growth, through an agricultural revolution that would raise agricultural productivity, transform the food sector, and create surpluses to feed the population.

Not only are these prescriptions in collision. Each one is pretty unworkable. Collective self-reliance and severance are fine on paper. In practice, if the ties between center and periphery are as strong as is often argued, the revolution that will break them is unlikely to prevail easily or widely. A study of Tanzanian self-reliance has shown that its trade with other Third World countries has not increased much.[39] Postrevolutionary socialist countries (those of Eastern Europe for instance) tend to relink with the outside world; China is going that direction also. On the other hand, as the radicals point out, the liberals' idea of fighting market imperfections is Sisyphean nonsense: the market itself breeds monopolies or oligopolies or cartels, and the privileged turn to the state for the protection of their advantages. As Fagen puts it, a state and a class analysis would show why the problems of poverty or national integration could not

be solved by "peripheric capitalism" even if the governments or the producers in the developing countries captured more of the national product.[40]
        Also, each set of prescriptions is blind to the problem of trade-offs. The radicals, in their hatred of dependency, are too ready to forget about growth: their ideal—while leading to a drastic decline in the living standards of the industrial powers, which they seem to wish—would still leave us with two worlds, a (less) advanced one, and a "delinked" developing one that would be more egalitarian within its boundaries, but would have given up the "lures" of growth for the joys of equity. (Especially with Galtung, we are never far from the Rousseauistic ideal of small communities as self-contained and pastoral as possible—an ideal modified only insofar as some transnational agencies are unavoidable.) Eager for growth, very few countries, whatever the rhetoric may be, have shown any particular desire for complete autarky and self-reliance. As one Russian economist once put it to me, self-reliant strategies would allow some of the underdeveloped countries, by themselves, to reach by the year 2300 the current economic level of Bulgaria. Another forgotten or implicitly sacrificed value is liberty: self-reliance, in practice, has been inseparable from repression—even in the Yugoslavia and China (Mao's China) Galtung admires. And the radicals fail to deal with problems of distributive justice within so-called socialist countries and within the socialist camp. Liberals, on the other hand, in their concern for growth and efficiency, either ignore the frequent contradictions between growth and equity or the frequent inefficiencies or wasteful aspects of capitalist development, or else rely on the uncertainties of trickle down, or count on state corrections without analyzing under what conditions the state has enough autonomy—at home and abroad—to carry them out.
        Finally, none of these rival visions is without its

contradictions. Many high priests of self-reliance nevertheless indict the advanced countries for closing their borders to competitive products from the developing ones, and denounce the protectionism of the developed nations just as they advocate much more of it for the poorer ones (Haq is a good example). But Western liberals, as Ajami has observed,[41] while pleading for the establishment of global norms of human rights, remain strictly noninterventionist in economic matters.

What, then, is to be done? Even if one leaves behind or pushes aside ideological visions and examines the suggestions of the more specialized literature on development in the hope of finding paths toward justice, one comes across difficulties of three kinds. First, some of the recommended solutions could actually make the problem worse. The liberals suggest that one place great hopes in a further and mutual liberalization of North-South trade. But if the radicals are right about the nature of the domestic and international capitalist economic systems, it cannot work that way. As Frances Stewart sees it, an intensification of this trade would only reenforce the advantage of the developed countries, because of the theory of cumulative causation.[42] If we turn to some of the suggestions made by the developing states, such as new and more favorable commodity agreements, should those commodity agreements jack up the prices, they would end up benefiting much more either the developed countries which produce these commodities, or the richer among the developing countries, or the owners of the resources within the developing countries, rather than the underdogs. As Amin puts it, a strategy aimed at obtaining higher prices for raw materials to finance industrialization would perpetuate unequal exchange—the poor would export goods produced with low wages—as well as a distorted pattern of demand and backward agriculture in the periphery. Moreover, the effect of such price increases may be regressive—at the expense of the poor—within the developed countries that import these goods.[43] If the agreements aim only at stabilizing prices, for instance through the creation of buffer stocks, this would not guarantee higher income from exports if the supply should greatly increase or demand fall. Nor would a link between Special Drawing Rights and development aid amount to the creation of new resources—and such a link might well be inflationary. The antipoverty campaign often recommended by Western radicals or reformers could not only slow growth but also increase the dependence of developing states, as long as they remain deprived of modern industries.[44] Generalized trade preferences have served as pretexts for the exclusion, by developed countries, of "sensitive" items, while the protection levels accorded to the developing countries have often safeguarded the production of inefficient and unessential goods.[45] And the proliferation of new international agencies to promote development in all its aspects could easily foster bureaucratic elephantiasis.[46] Or take the notion that one should make technology transfers more easy: if what is transferred is the wrong kind of technology, it is not going to help. Or the notion that one should make program lending more easy (which is one of the Brandt report's recommendations): if the money is wasted, it is not going to help either.

Secondly, some of the suggestions which are constantly made can be extraordinarily ambiguous in their effects; for instance, because of difficulties of targeting. Part of what one reads in most international reports is that the advanced countries should increase the flow of aid. But aid very often goes to those who are already better off, or preserves a dual economy instead of reducing inequality, or fosters the development of consumption rather than investment, or perpetuates dependence on the aid-giver, while giving him political leverage and preserving local elites in power.[47] Similarly, it is very difficult to target commodity agreements; many of them are not redistributive, many would benefit countries already receiving vast transfers of resources through trade and aid, and some are highly uncertain because of insufficient control of the market. Let us assume that the developed states are willing to share more power in international institutions with Third World countries. This may increase the bargaining power of the poor, but it may also multiply conflicts; it may make the institutions unmanageable.

Finally, while some of the suggestions sound very good, they would be effective only if they were accompanied by drastic change far beyond the current international processes. As we have seen, many authors suggest a huge antipoverty effort. Not only would it require vast resources, but such a campaign by the rich to lift the level of the poor entails the most drastic kind of interventionism. How is this going to be accomplished? Moreover, as Robert Cox has pointed out, if "world capitalism tends to perpetuate itself and to continually recreate the inequalities of uneven development," according to the radicals' critique, "a basic needs approach that did not attack the issue of tranforming world economic structures would be condemned to failure," or to providing for the poor a mere "welfare counterpart to capitalist development."[48] The sensible and important suggestion, which is made by Arthur Lewis and by Jan Tinbergen, that what is needed above all is an increase in agricultural productivity in the poor countries, cannot be carried out in many countries unless land is redistributed—latifundia are to be broken up, or exccssively small parcels put together. But such profound structural reforms affecting land, irrigation schemes, and food production in the developing countries require a major political upheaval. Similarly, it is often suggested—by Brandt as well as by Griffin—that one needs the participation of the poor themselves in local decision-making. This too would amount to a revolution. How can one provoke—and channel—it from the outside? Such are the difficulties.

And yet we must provide some principles to guide us in our search for elements of a solution. Nothing would be easier than to draft one's own utopia: this is what most books and reports in this field amount to— they are acts of faith on a thin tightrope of hopes without any net under them. I am not saying this in condemnation: exhortation or indoctrination is the only weapon of those who, devoid of power, try to influence the statesmen. But my effort, here as in the previous chapter, consists in trying to suggest how far one can go realistically on the road toward the ideal. When, as here, we find disagreements on the nature of injustice, on its roots, and on the remedies, when a fairly detached observer can only conclude that each view contains if not a kernel of truth, at least an excellent critique of the other views' weaknesses, then his own recommendations cannot help but be somewhat messy.

Indeed, the first principle I would pose is the need for eclecticism. We cannot advocate a strategy aimed exclusively at meeting basic human needs because for instance, "no Northern government has both the credibility and the resources to launch and lead such a program seriously and globally,"[49] and because of the difficulties of enforcing it "in a world in which many recipient governments are corrupt, indifferent to mass welfare, or guilty of aggressive or irresponsible behavior"; therefore, in Rothstein's words, "acceptance of the principle of need is neither feasible nor necessarily more just than a system based on a combination of different allocation principles."[50] We do not have to choose between basic needs and the issues of trade or commodity development or institutional reform raised by Third World governments. Nor do we have to choose between efficiency and equity: the kind of growth often praised by liberals is neither equitable nor efficient, if by efficiency one means the rational use of all available resources, including those of the land and of the potential, often unemployed, workers. "What is good for equality may be good for efficiency," in the Third World as well as in developed states; "there is a long way to go before hitting the real trade-off zone."[51] The use of appropriate technologies, the development of health and education, the efforts of some countries such as Taiwan or South Korea to improve income distribution have led to vast gains in efficiency.[52] Nor can we endorse a clear choice between delinking and fuller participation in an open international economy. Total interdependence is unbearable, for the weak even more than for the strong, total self-reliance is stultifying. There are serious disadvantages if either strategy is pushed to the extreme; once more a mix is needed. As Lewis recommends, the developing countries could trade more with each other and thus reduce their dependence on developed countries for trade, but he recognizes that total severance from the latter is impossible as long as the basic reform of agriculture he wants has not been achieved and there has been no switch in "engines of growth." And the developing countries can gain vital resources by playing the game of the international economy, provided the latter is reformed to reduce the built-in advantages of the developed countries. Many states of the Third World have achieved gains by a strategy of industrialization for exports; many of them have called in foreign investment for this purpose; they have minimized the risks of dependence by exploiting their own countervailing power once the multinationals were installed[53] and by fostering local competition to the foreign enterprises. Conversely, even a radical like Allende kept trying to obtain international credits: self-reliance was forced on him by American policy; and Haq calls for vast resource transfers to finance investments in domestic energy production in oil-importing developing countries.[54]

In dealing with interstate relations, there are a number of measures which the richer states (including the oil-rich countries with small populations) should take and which are both prudent and just, insofar as the Third World states can be seen as the guardians and the promoters of their own peoples. ("Insofar" is a restrictive formula.) I refer to the various measures proposed by economists like Fishlow, Cooper, or Miriam Camps,[55] for helping remove barriers to the exports of the manufactured products of underdeveloped countries, and for mutual guarantees of access to markets. Miriam Camps suggests that actions taken by a country which affect others—most protectionist devices in the advanced countries and in the new industrial countries that are the richest in the developing world fall in this category—be seen as being of legitimate international concern. I also refer to many recommendations aimed at easier access of the poor states to long-term financing, at constituting buffer stocks to stabilize the fluctuations of commodity prices, or at reaching agreements based on the European community model to guarantee the level of earnings derived from the export of commodities by Third World countries. The joint exploitation of commons, like the resources of the oceans, would provide important financial resources for development. Such measures are derived from considerations of mutual interest (short and long term on the side of the developing countries, sometimes only long term on that of the developed ones); but security of access, a stabilization of commodity prices that would dampen both inflation and recession, a program of international food reserves aimed at preventing both famines and wild price fluctuations, and an increase in the purchasing power of Third World markets which have become, in the 70's, the latest growing source of trade for the developed countries, all these concerns are valid in the short run also. Indeed, several of these measures might improve prospects for greater distributive justice within the richer countries, given their dependence on the international economy.

As for an international regime for foreign investment, the importance of the issue is itself controversial. If one believes, as both the radicals and the liberals do, that multinational corporations are very important instruments indeed, for good in the liberal view and for bad in the radical view, then the issue is of fundamental significance. If, like Arthur Lewis, one believes that they do not make much difference, that their importance has been much exaggerated, and that there will be less and less direct investment in the poorer countries as years go by, the issue loses in salience, and all the energy spent on highly elastic codes is somewhat wasted. Whatever one's opinion, this is an area of mutual interests. Many of the governments of developing countries, given the choices they have made of models of development, are eager for the multinational corporations to come in, create jobs, and increase production and trade. And in many such countries business is still profitable enough for the corporations to have an interest in moving there. International codes by themselves are probably not the best means of dealing with the problems. They can provide a framework for case-by-case bargaining; from the viewpoint of the Third or Fourth World countries, the first imperative is for the state itself to be in enough of a position of power to be able to bargain with the multinationals on a foot of relative equality. If the relation is that which existed between United Fruit and a banana republic, there is no bargain possible. On the other hand, if it is the relation which exists in many of the Latin American countries and in some of the Asian ones, it is much more even.

Similarly, in the regulation of the oceans, the advanced countries need the consent of Third World countries to institute any kind of order. The capitalist nations could just send their technology to mine the seabeds without waiting for the consent of the hundred and so nations which have not given it so far. But there would be complete chaos fairly rapidly, and a probable extension of state rights and controls by the developing countries over other parts of the oceans. It is precisely the rich who have the greatest interest in order and predictability, because that is what their economies need; they have an interest in getting the consent of the poorer states. And many of the latter have an interest in not producing world chaos. During the international economic crisis of the early 70's, even the communist countries were not eager to see the final crisis of capitalism arrive, insofar as they were deriving certain benefits from the system also. This mutuality of interests puts limits both on the possibility of preserving the status quo and on the amount of upheaval that states really want to go through. This is why, if one looks at the various negotiations that are going on, there is such an enormous difference between the rhetoric on both sides and the practical arrangements that one arrives at in the end, and which marginally do change a little of something.

Also in the realm of interstate justice, it is—for the same reasons—in the interest of developed countries to meet the demands of the Third World for greater participation in collective decision-making. Here, compromises between efficiency and broad participation have to be found—the model of the UN General Assembly, or of UNCTAD, is not inspiring. But the suggestions in the Brandt report for a reform of the World Bank and the I.M.F., and Miriam Camps's ingenious scheme for a new global trade organization with a variety of boards where membership would vary, are valuable.

Since Third World states—like the states of developed countries—are often massively imperfect, they cannot be the only concern of a moral policy of distributive justice. In the transfer of resources to them which would result from these measures or from continuing aid, we must find a balance between predictability, important for the Third World (it is bad to have aid submitted to internal debate in the U.S. every year), and performance. The notion proposed by a number of reformist and social democratic authors, and endorsed by the Brandt report, that aid should be made more automatic, has to be qualified. Automaticity in the raising of revenues is a desirable goal, automaticity in their transfer to recipient states is not. As one Third World writer, Ali Mazrui, put it, this kind of automaticity or the absence of strings exists only in the form of charity. "Equality implies exchange" among equals, "any transfer of resources ... must always be conditional on some kind of a quid pro quo."[56] But performance—what we want them to do in exchange— ought to be defined much less in the terms of classical economics, the terms imposed by the I.M.F. or the Chicago school, which would actually decrease aid to the poorest, and much more in terms of distributive justice. The developed countries ought to see to it that food aid reaches the hungry, and that the benefits from the transfer of resources reach those who are worse off in the developing countries, and particularly in the poorer countries that would benefit least from new trade or commodity deals.[57] This would entail a commitment by the richer countries to help launch a variety of projects in fields such as health, water and soil management, food production, transport and communications, and to provide the necessary credits to finance payments deficits, for the poorest nations. Such a commitment would, in the long run, require these countries' consent to an incipient system of international taxation (many suggestions have been made, ranging from an income tax to levies on arm exports, on the exploitation of seabed minerals, or armaments, or on the extraction of natural resources). But justice also dictates that the advanced countries should try to use the mutuality of interests which exists between them and developing ones in order to obtain from the latter that they go beyond mere interstate justice and look after the basic needs of their people. If one leaves those needs to the domestic markets of the Third World as they are, they will not be met. It may sound like blackmail, but in blackmail cases one of the actors is doing something illegitimate or selfish. There is a wrong and a right kind of mutuality. Since all of the Third World governments want something from the richer countries, there is no reason why the latter countries cannot ask for something—unselfish—in exchange. Automatically transferred multilateral aid would not serve the long-term interests of the people who are badly treated, or live in poverty, or are victimized in any other way, even if it satisfied the ego of the governments. That is why the distinction between state and individual is important, and why one has to remember that the states should be taken seriously as partners only insofar as the presumption that they speak for their people has not been destroyed.

But we have to remember that we cannot reach those poorer people directly: we have to work through the states as they are, which is not easy; also, we cannot launch an antipoverty campaign in the developing world without the consent of its highly suspicious governments fearful that such a campaign would be a pretext for avoiding all the other measures they are interested in;

and therefore we would have a chance only if we clearly did not separate the two fronts, so to speak, but instead used interstate negotiations as a lever to try to get the condition of individuals improved. There will be cries of intervention, but as Fagen points out, development aid—eagerly sought by many states—was always interventionist. Clearly, Third World governments prefer trade and commodity negotiations, which, if successful, provide them with greater resources they can use as they please. Precisely, new agreements in those areas should be made conditional on the adoption by these governments of measures aimed at internal equity.

A second principle is the need for perspective. All of what I have advocated so far looks disappointing—meager or uncertain in its results. But there are other ways in which one can contribute to distributive justice. Internationally, one can promote it not only by taking seriously those parts of the demands for a new international economic order that deserve to be taken seriously, but also, outside of the economic realm, by doing something about the arms race. The Brandt report gives fascinating figures on how much it costs to build a tank, by comparison with how much aid is being given. Even within the realm of economics one can do a great deal for distributive justice, outside the negotiations for a new international economic order, for instance by providing a more stable and less inflationary international monetary system (which has not been the case for some years), or better coordinated management of the economies of the developed countries.

Above all, our greatest contribution to international distributive justice will have to come from domestic measures. There is no substitute for domestic action, either by the rich nations or by the poor ones. International measures of the kind I have described have limited possibilities. If all those measures were taken in interstate negotiations, all they would do is make the less developed states capable of adopting a style of development that would promote equity; but that is all. The ultimate responsibility is on domestic measures. In the less developed countries, domestic reform could enormously enhance their position in the North-South negotiations.[58] There is much to be learned from the radical analysis, or from Lewis' analysis. Lewis stresses that the potential for growth of the less developed countries exists already, and would be unaffected "even if all the developed countries were to sink into the sea,"[59] (which he says he does not thereby recommend). Domestic measures have to be taken by each developing country itself. They cannot wait until (although their effectiveness could be magnified by) the reform and improvement of the external framework in which these states operate. Domestic action very often would mean radical change. It is of course true that the elites of these countries have no interest in reforming themselves out of power or out of existence: the agrarian revolution called for by Lewis, the switch in development models advocated by radicals (often fascinated by the China of the cultural revolution and gang of four, not by the current China in which a bureaucratic elite consolidates its power) would entail either a mass conversion at the top or an upheaval from below. My point is that without such changes, international measures will remain incomplete.

Domestic measures by the developed countries are just as important. We will never move toward justice (at home or abroad) if we follow the logic of zero growth. Growth is needed because otherwise there will be no resources to transfer to or to distribute in the poorer countries, no willingness to raise such resources, a growing imbalance between resources and population, and a jungle of protectionist barriers. Not only do we have a duty of growth, which can only be carried out by domestic effort, but also a duty to avoid recessions, because recessions engender protectionism, they spread, and are fatal to the possibilities of trade and industrialization of other countries. We have a duty to conserve energy, because otherwise the increase in the cost of imported oil will drive the poorer oil-importing countries into bankruptcy and the accumulation of money reserves by the oil producers will further endanger the international monetary and banking systems. And we—along with the oil-producing developing countries—have a duty to do all we can to curb inflation, which raises the cost of imports of oil and of other goods by the poorer nations and, like depressions, forces them often into astronomical debt, thus threatening the whole international financial mechanism. Finally if we believe our own arguments about a lasting mutual interest in developing North-South trade—that is, in opening our borders more widely to exports from the developing nations—it is essential that we take internal measures of "adjustment," a familiar euphemism for envisaging and carrying out a transfer of activity and resources from enterprises that are no longer competitive to new, more advanced sectors.

Not surprisingly, the third principle is the need for modesty. Insisting on the domestic measures that have to be taken already indicates that, in my opinion, full distributive justice is beyond international relations. Much of what we do through international relations is half blind, because we really do not know the effects of what we are doing. It is pleasant and easy to say, "Transfer resources," but when people start arguing whether those resources should help raise the consumption of the poor today, or boost investments today so that there will be no poor tomorrow, nobody really knows which course is better in itself, there are fervent advocates of both, and the impact varies from place to place.[60] Much of what we do through international relations is much more prudential than moral—let us face it. I have repeatedly said that moral politics combines the prudential with the moral. But this does not mean that all that is done for prudential reasons is *ipso facto* moral, nor that it is undertaken out of a sense of duty—it is done either for circumstantial reasons, or out of what I have called Machiavellian state morality. And much of what we do through international relations is, as we have seen, at least as capable of worsening the situation as of solving anything, precisely because the market is what it is.

So I come to an unhappy first conclusion, which is that while distributive justice is no longer purely an internal concern, our external reach is limited. In the absence of supranational institutions and of transnational consensus, the international politics of distributive justice are bound to be frustrating—the result of hard bargains between states for whom power or status are certainly as important as justice, and of a tug of war between well-meaning reformers trying to reach the poor across the barriers of state borders, and governments eager to preserve both their nation's independence and their domestic power base. Never is this more the case than in a period when the developed countries are struggling with low growth, high inflation, and high unemployment simultaneously, when their opinions are seduced by conservative or jingoistic sirens, when, in other words, both the resources and the will for justice abroad are missing. At such moments the gap between the climate of world affairs and even such authoritative exhortations as, say, the Brandt report—with its countless "shoulds," its call for an international system of universal revenue mobilization and for extensive schemes of international taxation[61]—is an abyss.

Conversely, and this is a second discouraging conclusion, domestic distributive justice in the real world is permanently problematic. Internally, the eternal debate between reformers and radicals goes on, with the radicals arguing that mere reforms never go to the root of things and often prolong agony interminably, that the root of the evil is in the nature of the system, and that the whole system must be destroyed and replaced. But the radicals split into two camps. The utopians never explain either how their dream of small, communelike, quasi-self-sufficient communities matches the universal experience of group selfishness (either in mutual relations or in the delicate balance between what can be enjoyed now and what must be laid aside for tomorrow), or how that dream and their design for central planning bodies can be reconciled without coercion, or—above all—how universal populism will reach Erewhon or Nirvana without colossal turmoil. The revolutionaries, at least, do not shrink from violence; but the reformers answer that a revolution normally breaks so many eggs that one is likely to get a bloodbath and a new tyranny. There may be greater equity, and greater progress in the realm of health care, housing, or employment, in the communist world; but nonfunctional inequalities still abound, there are serious problems of distributive justice within a hierarchical camp or within the Soviet system of nationalities, and the trade-offs are intolerable. This debate has been raging for centuries. Internationally, the same kind of debate goes on. Reformism risks either being unheeded because even the changes it advocates are too explosive for the guardians of the local status quo—who all know that repressive regimes unravel when reforms begin or repression relents: remember the French and the Iranian revolutions—or else being so superficial as to perpetuate an unjust status quo. On the other hand, a wave of domestic revolutions aimed at greater egalitarianism could be entirely destructive of international relations, while impeding the international pursuit of distributive justice. Would the United States support, financially and economically, countries that had all established socialist regimes which would almost inevitably be anti-American?[62] Furthermore, if one of the requirements of ethical politics is a moderate world order, can there be a moderate order composed largely of revolutionary states trying to reach equality at home by extremely drastic means? Does not recent experience in Southeast Asia show that this would entail both a revival of ethnic hatreds among revolutionary states, each one intent on pursuing its own salvation, and a most dangerous opportunity for great power interventions and rivalries?

It is between these rocks, or icebergs, or shoals, that we must navigate. In the chapter on human rights, I used the relatively rosy image of turning a circle into a spiral. In matters of distributive justice the appropriate metaphor would be Sisyphus and his rock—or De Gaulle's more military one, which he applied to economics, of a battlefield on which the sun of Austerlitz never rises.[63] If death defines the human condition, injustice defines the social one. There is a duty, national and international, to reduce it as much as possible. But there is no definitive victory.

An Ethics of World Order

THE PROBLEM OF WORLD ORDER

READERS WHO followed this road so far may well feel that we have been chasing a mirage. Are not the possibilities of moral foreign policy so limited, is not the realm of international relations so unrewarding—both because of the fundamental constraints described in the first chapter and because of the specific features of the three subjects analyzed in the next three—that we end up, each time, with only little hope, and uncertain directions?

It is indeed a frustrating journey. But this could not be avoided once we had chosen as our approach what Arnold Wolfers many years ago called "a nonperfectionist, nonnationalist ethic."[1] It takes the world as it is, both as a point of departure and as the material to work not just on but with (there is a nuance). Applied ethics is not the province of the ethical philosopher, it is the domain of the student of the given field of application—as long as this student cares about moral issues. The nature of international politics dictates that moral action should be altogether capable of accommodating a large diversity of values in the world, be both interstate and cosmopolitan, be compatible with the (enlightened) interests of the states (because otherwise it would never be effective), and consist of partly utilitarian, partly categorical rules. We all know that no "ought" can be simply and directly de-

rived from an "is." What we have now tells us how difficult it is to go beyond—indeed, how easily things might
get worse. It does not tell us where we ought to go. What I
have tried, sketchily, is to suggest some directions, derived from a certain moral conception, and defined by
my sense of the possible—shaped, in other words, by my
view of the interplay between moral norms and political
realities.

       In this conception of moral obligation, states have
two kinds of moral ends. The first consists of legitimate
self-regarding ones: the promotion of the long-term
interests of the national community, in a way that avoids
or at least minimizes harm to those of other national
communities. The second category comprises other-
regarding goals, both with respect to the society of states
(preservation of the balance of power, resistance against
aggression, protection of economic interdependence—
which does not mean that it must be made or kept so
intense, or so uneven, as to be unbearable to some participants) and with respect to foreign human beings (defense of their human rights; distributive justice, etc.).
These goals can be deduced from the "legalist paradigm"
described in Chapter 2, and from those moral and political conditions of internal legitimacy that have already
become, and ought to become even more in the future,
matters of international concern. A policy aimed at such
goals would reconcile the moral and the national interests, or rather define the national interest in moral terms.
To clarify (or complicate) things one more time, I repeat
that morality is not merely a matter of ends or intentions,
and that the likely consequences of acts must be taken
into account (a principle such as resistance to aggression
could otherwise become a recipe for the generalization or
escalation of conflict, as dangerous as the "Munich
analogy")—especially when the goal is ambiguous, or the
principle to be applied is slippery (as, for instance, self-
determination so often is). But, on the other hand, a

morality that relies exclusively on expected, calculated outcomes is not acceptable either: no statesman can be sure of all effects, and confident that he will be able to avoid perverse ones altogether. Neither pure conviction nor unbridled "consequentialism" will do.

This approach, which aims at realism, nevertheless refuses to accept or to sanctify the world as it is. Hence the term, "nonnationalistic." It recognizes that there is a need to go beyond what we have now. The traditional "morality" of foreign policy, the Machiavellian one, is unacceptable both on intellectual grounds—it is based on a conception of international "state of war" that is not the permanent reality—and on moral ones—to follow its precepts could turn international politics into such a state of war, and leave little room for improvement. Under certain conditions, or in certain cases, the contest of states relaxes sufficiently to make improvement possible. It is therefore our duty to seek it and to work to establish such conditions. This is the problem of world order. I accept Hedley Bull's definition of it: "Those patterns or dispositions of human activity that sustain the elementary or primary goals of social life among mankind as a whole";[2] he is right to point out that it is wider, more fundamental, and morally prior to order among states. Bull and others have pointed out that international order, or order among states, has often been unjust and, I would add, indifferent to human rights as well as as either casual or largely unsuccessful in trying to limit violence. Past schemes of international order, in other words, have, first, been unconcerned with the dimensions of world order that go beyond interstate affairs—these realms were left to transnational society, at best—and, secondly, amounted to no more than attempts at reconciling, or at organizing the coexistence of Machiavellian moralities—at making the state of war bearable. This is simply not enough.

But the difficulty of the approach taken here is

that while it aims at going beyond past attempts at order among states, it starts from the states as they are and recognizes that their games, lethal as they may be, cannot be wished away: hence the term, "nonperfectionist." This approach rejects what has been for many years a rather important Anglo-American (and, in the postwar era, primarily American) tradition, now represented by Richard Falk and his associates of the World Order Models Project. It is a utopian tradition that can be faulted on two grounds; first of all, the ground of feasibility or rather unfeasibility. Their approach is quite incapable of describing adequately how one gets from here to there. Of course they try, but they do reach their goal by pure arbitrariness. One of the authors, in a recent book, explains that world reform will come by the creation of what is called in his book a planetary citizens' movement, whose members would "bind themselves to their view of a preferred world future and develop a consensus-building yet nondoctrinaire global belief system."[3] He does not explain how the values of global humanism, which he espouses, would overcome national hatreds and prejudices, or the obstacles erected by so many regimes that show no fondness for citizens' movements at all. The same apolitical bent characterizes another author, who envisages a global community of small societies, but who leaves us in the dark about how to transform today's world of "structural violence" into tomorrow's ideal, perhaps because in his obsession with center-periphery relations he takes practically no account of the resilience of nations.[4] The same can be said of still another author, who suggests that reform should consist of reducing the number of states in the world to about twenty-five.[5] Again, how does he propose to do this? In all these instances, unfeasibility derives from a kind of surface antinationalism: It is not just an anationalistic or a non-nationalist ethic; it is an antinationalist one which finds something radically wrong in, and therefore wants to do away with, what exists, that is, what one has to work with.

Secondly, this approach rests also on a kind of moral arrogance—a readiness to paint the world in two colors only, the black of present structures or of present elites, and the white of the utopia in which the authors' values will prevail. Insofar as several of these writers are American, for all of their good will they seem to evince a profoundly American characteristic: their anti-nationalism relies on or derives from a particularly engaging brand of American nationalism, not the nationalism of expansion or conquest that one often encounters in other countries, nor the "exceptionalist" American nationalism that sees the United States as the sheriff of a troubled world, but the other brand of exceptionalism which dreams of an America that would be the champion of enlightened progress, the missionary who uplifts those less advanced or less fortunate—a brand of self-righteousness that smacks, like its counterpart, of the tyranny of benevolence and of naïveté: If only our government were as good as our people, and if only everybody could be like us, there would be no problems. It is assumed here that the good ethical values are so self-evident, and are so much in the political and moral interest of all, that the millennium will come, of course. This leads to the postulate that if only we, the privileged and (potentially) good, made certain fundamental changes of attitude, if only we did away with weapons or shared our wealth, for instance, we could all by ourselves, by the force of example, bring the world to Nirvana. At the root of this approach lies the old liberal hubris about how education and enlightenment and virtue are all rolled into one. In a way, I envy the writers of this school, because they have a very easy task—when they meet an obstacle they just describe it away.

The problem of world order, envisaged from the viewpoint of an ethics that is neither utopian nor Machiavellian, is both essential and elusive. It is essential because, as indicated above, world order is nothing other than the set of processes and procedures, the global regime, that makes ethical foreign policy action possible. But it is elusive for a multitude of reasons. First, it is profoundly different from domestic order, which rests on a consensus of values or on the authority of the central institutions; here a (minimal) consensus, and the development of adequate institutions, are goals, not foundations. Secondly, there is something circular (optimists would say cumulative) about the process of world order; the imperatives I have suggested in dealing with force, human rights and distributive justice would constitute part of those "patterns or dispositions" that Bull alludes to, but it is only under certain conditions that these norms have a chance of being adopted and effective. On the other hand, clearly, should nations and citizens follow them, the establishment and consolidation of these conditions would be greatly helped.

Thirdly, as we have seen, statesmen and citizens, in order to promote world order have at their disposal only two kinds of actions that have a chance of effectiveness. They can practice unilateral restraint, or they can cooperate on collective measures. When we discussed force and human rights, we saw that much evil could be avoided by unilateral restraint. But restraint has two sharp limits: first, as long as it is exercised only by a handful of actors, and especially not by the major ones, its effects will be modest. A statesman who follows imperatives of restraint may feel that he had done his moral duty, but his contribution to world order may be far smaller than his contribution to his nation's moral stature. Moveover, restraint is often fragile if it is not reciprocated by the actor's chief competitor(s): security, survival, and the other concerns tied to the contest of states, will threaten restraint when one reaches the famous threshold of supreme necessity, or when restraint proves ineffective or insufficiently effective and appears to give an advantage to an unrestrained adversary. When we discussed human rights and distributive justice, we concluded that the best chances of effectiveness depended on cooperation—on what is often called coalition—building. But (we return to the previous point, circularity) the chances for this depend in turn on the prerequisite of incipient world order, or enough of an agreement on its outlines, or on the perils of disorder, to allow for broad bargaining and collaboration.

Fourth, if we look at world order as both the sum of moral foreign policy actions and the condition for their possibility, nothing is more important yet difficult than coherence. Every major decision a stateman makes has a moral dimension, insofar as it affects people's lives, or their ability to pursue happiness, well-being, or their ideals and beliefs. But the ethics of international affairs cannot be simply an ethics of disconnected decisions, each one made on its own merits. Every one of those choices involves some trade-offs, and unless statesmen have an overall sense of direction, their individual decisions can lead absolutely nowhere, or even be disastrous. Precisely because the ethics of politics is an ethics of consequences, each decision has ripples; in the absence of a map and a compass, incoherence will have some fairly destructive effects even on the bits and pieces with which the moral politician has to concern himself. Coherence requires a proper balance between the intractably confrontational aspects of international politics—the dictates of Machiavellian ethics, if you like—and the aspiration for a better order (precisely what utopians neglect). Coherence also requires a constant balancing of all the "goods" in collision. In recent years the foreign policy of the Carter administration has suffered from an inability to provide these balances. First, the aspirations seemed to shoot too far ahead of the confrontations; second, among the various worthy goals: non-proliferation, restraints on arms sales, better North-South relations, the promotion of human rights, East-West détente, etc., there seemed to occur more of the kinds of collisions one observes in pinball machines, than of the ordering of priorities one expects of statecraft. In the abstract there is no way of prescribing priorities: it all depends on the hierarchy of perils and on that of possibilities, and these vary from place to place and from moment to moment. But coherence requires at least two things: a clear sense of what the greatest dangers are—an ordered and graduated list of the unacceptables, so to speak; and an awareness of the fact that the pursuit of any one value, be it peace or distributive justice at the expense of other values, liberty, or of the necessities of the contest, military balance, for instance, leads to calamities. The fake coherence that results from the unbalanced attempt to maximize only one value at the expense of the others is as sure to backfire as the attempt to run after all of them at once without a strategy. All good things do not come together; but a concentration on one to the detriment of the others is not the answer.

This problem of coherence is a particular challenge for the approach I have suggested, which is a liberal or a reformist approach. It is not a problem for the perfect utopian, or the utopian perfectionist à la Falk, who posits five or ten values and builds a mirage in which they all shine, nor is it a problem for the revolutionary. He has the great advantage of explaining why the present is necessarily bad, and since it is bad, he often feels extremely free to justify for its destruction the use of what other people might call rather dubious methods. But he justifies them by subordinating the creation of a morally satisfactory world to the triumph of the revolution, or by postponing it until after that triumph. I have stated before that many domestic revolutions have struck me as unavoidable or positive, on balance, in their results. But from the viewpoint of world order, the problem with the revolutionary vision is double—it concerns both today and tomorrow. Today we face the old dilemma of dirty hands; in the debate between Camus and Sartre in the early 50's, Camus said that the means one uses today shape the ends that one might perhaps reach tomorrow. Anyhow, the world as it is at present is much too fragile for the shock tactics of revolutionaries if (as so often happens) these tactics get exported, for instance through terrorism, or invite the interventions of outsiders. And the problem for tomorrow is that revolutionary thought suffers from two flaws in envisaging an ideal world. One is—again—utopianism. Revolutionary thought is extraordinarily cheerful about how things will be after the triumph and spread of revolution. Suddenly we will be a world unlike anything human nature has ever known in the past: no wars for conquest, no exploitation, no imperialism, new human beings. Not only is this utopian, but there are violent battles among revolutionaries on what the utopia ought to look like. There are now about as many schools of socialism as one can imagine. Those who advocate peripheric socialism and the break-up of the center are not those who believe that the "socialism" already established at the center—in Moscow—must be the model for future revolutions. And there is a cacophony of peripheral models as well.

   A liberal, or reformist, approach to world order plays all the cards against itself. Not only does it recognize the plurality of values to be pursued and the contradictions that ensue, but it also acknowledges the divergences among states (and among citizens) when it comes either to interpreting those values or to ranking them.

Moreover, it knows that in a world of competing states the best approximation to order ever achieved was the balance of power, which represented not a repudiation of the Machiavellian "morality of struggle" but merely an attempt at moderating the struggle, so as to allow the principal powers to pursue selfish policies with a modicum of security and predictability. Insofar as protracted peace, or only limited wars among the great powers resulted from the attempt, this was a point of contact or convergence between Machiavellian ethics and the "nonnationalist, nonperfectionist ethics" advocated here. (Machiavellian morality is Janus-like. One face is the ethics of the state of war, of public safety, survival and necessity, of unexamined friends and of foes treated as such without qualms, precisely because of the risks and costs of life and death situations; there is another face, the ethos of balance of power systems, with their coalitions and compromises, their compensations and their restraints.) A moderate international system is both the outcome of the balance of power (when it functions properly), and the precondition for the far more ambitious kind of ethical world order, for the more demanding kinds of ethical foreign policies, that are my concern. For the latter aims at the achievement, at the global level and through the moves of the actors on the world scene, of essential human rights and aspirations. And these will remain unfulfilled (even though, as we have shown repeatedly, their realization depends in the first place on the domestic regime) as long as the international system is marked by injustice, tolerance for violations of basic human rights, and a multitude of preparations for and resorts to force, which always open the floodgates to further domestic infringements of rights. The problem of world order is how to move toward so ambitious a goal—without a precooked model of world government—in a world so fragmented and dangerous that world order appears simultaneously indispensable and unreachable—through the operations of the very actors whose behavior, at home and abroad, is the source of injustice, violence and repression.

I have tried in a recent book to describe a policy of world order that would be in the interest of the United States.[6] I will not repeat my arguments here. Instead, and taking into account the discouraging experiences of the past few years, I will present some additional thoughts first about the interstate system, and then about specific groups of persons whose moves can affect world affairs.

THE INTERSTATE SYSTEM

A first series of remarks concerns the urgency of the attempt to define ethical-political conditions of world order; a second set of remarks concerns the execution of such a policy.

In the past, what one found in many treatises about world affairs (especially in American thinking, or in Anglo-American thinking) was first of all a defense of incrementalism, and secondly, the ideal which is a lodestar for many of the best authors in the field of international relations, Hans Morgenthau or E. H. Carr or Hedley Bull or Kenneth Waltz, the ideal of moderation. Neither is quite enough anymore. I don't mean to suggest that we should call for global reform, in one fell swoop. Piecemeal change, gradual advances, are the best we can expect. But we need a sense of direction, a concern for the long term—not mere muddling through from day to day. It is always tempting for a moral statesman, or a statesman who sees himself as moral, to fall back on politics as usual. It is the present president of the French Republic who, with singular and somewhat uncharacteristic modesty, defined the art of the statesman as managing the unforeseeable. In other words, one must navigate the best one can between the daily Scyllas and Charybdises. This is not adequate at all. It may be the best one succeeds in doing, but it certainly should not be one's plan. In the past, managing the unforeseeable has never prevented the final collapse of moderate international systems for precisely the reason which was analyzed in the sharpest way by Rousseau two centuries ago: the ultimate incompatibility of interests, especially in matters of life and death. Not only has it never really worked in the past, but incrementalism is not reassuring at all in the present, especially, of course, because of the existence of nuclear weapons and all of the catastrophes—physical, moral, political—that would result from their possible use, and because of the enormous magnitude of the problems of the international economy. We have already discussed some of the problems of the poor, but there is also, pretty visibly, the disarray of the rich. Never before have there been so many states, of which a majority are powderkegs because of internal heterogeneity, or political repression, or economic deprivation. Nor is incrementalism reassuring at a time of increasing difficulties for crisis management which result either from the problems of violent conflict (interstate or intrastate) or from the problems of the economy, and even more—as we see in the Middle East—from the interplay between the two. An American diplomat, a few years ago, writing about the oil crisis—before October '73—wrote an article called "This Time the Wolf Is Here."[7] This could be said about international crises in general. In the past, the worst that could happen if something went wrong in the game was that some of the players might get bumped off, but the game would continue. This time, the game itself is threatened with self-destruction.

The last reason why incrementalism does not

work has to do with a fundamental fact. The chief actors in the world as we know it are still the states. The expectation one might have had in the past, when one was slightly optimistic, that state interests somehow could converge by trial and error—an expectation which incidentally was proven false even when there was a genuine family of states, when the leaders belonged more or less to the same class or mental universe—is now completely unrealistic. The world is full of life and death situations. If one looks at the European system of 1914, one finds one major power which was clearly in such a situation and knew it—Austria-Hungary. The present world is full of Austria-Hungary's. Think of the ethnic and religious conflicts that plague many Asian states. For such tottering countries, the outside world is either a threat or a tempting prey for diversion. Also, the international system is much more heterogenous than at any other moment; not only in terms of ideologies, but also in the sense that there is a radical difference between states run by secular churches, where power rests on a kind of fusion of physical control and legitimizing dogma, and all the others, or in the sense that states behave as if they did belong to different ages of international affairs. The new states which have just acceded at least to the appearance of sovereignty have a way of acting as if state behavior of the eighteenth and nineteenth centuries was still the norm (even when they show great skill at building cartels or coalitions to enhance their interests). Some of the older states—not all of them—are beginning to be a bit more sober. A last reason why this convergence of states' interests cannot be expected is that the states now have domestic functions that are much bigger, more ambitious, more sweeping, more invading of society (even if one takes as the only yardstick the percentage of the GNP which the state consumes), than ever before. However, in most cases, they have much less control of the instruments of policy, less autonomy in carrying out these functions than ever before; this is particularly true in the advanced liberal or capitalist states, but not exclusively. Many of the traditional tools of power which they did enjoy are no longer at their disposal at all—the economic ones have been blunted by interdependence and its boomerangs, the military ones are often too sharp to be used safely—and many of the new states, once they have achieved sovereignty and independence, discover that these are purely *pro forma*. Frustration is far more likely to lead to frantic attempts at preserving whatever autonomy is left, or at exploiting fully the national tools still available, than to the harmonization of partial impotencies. Moreover, convergence or harmony are particularly unlikely between those few states that are reasonably self-sufficient, and all the others.

What about moderation? In the past there was always a debate among authors on how to deal with the problem of force; the utopians preached quite simply the abolition of the "war system," and the others answered that the best one could do was to dampen violence, as the balance of power did. Similarly, in the discussion of the problem of want, a debate still goes on, as we saw, between those who see in it above all a problem of interstate accommodation, and those who think that the only truly satisfactory answers must be global equity solutions, going far beyond intergovernmental agreements. Still, in each of these two cases the prevailing wisdom, which the statesmen have accepted, has always been on the milder side of the alternative—moderation rather than abolition of force, and interstate rather than global equity in economic affairs. At present, for reasons we have tried to discuss, one cannot be quite so smug. When one examines the problem of force, the answer should be that one has to find a way of pushing moderation beyond what it meant in the past, moving gradually toward abolition (while realizing full well that it isn't exactly going to happen tomorrow); and similarly, one has to get somewhere in-between interstate compacts and global equity solutions in the realm of distributive justice. The significance of this is that if one wants to create the political conditions of world order, one has to act simultaneously on three different levels of turmoil. The obstacles to moral action result—fundamentally— from the absence in the international milieu of a legitimate monopoly of force (that is, from the states' resort to force), from the absence of consensus, and— concretely—from the specific causes of conflict. First, one has to work on the level of force itself; here two things are required, which sometimes clash. The first is the imperative of "crime shall not pay." As we know, there will never be any kind of order if states get away with aggression; this does create certain moral imperatives in areas such as deterrence, defense, and collective security. In other words, as again Wolfers pointed out, even if one wants to move international relations from the pole of hostility to the pole of greater friendship, it cannot be friendship as appeasement. But at the same time there also has to be much more of an effort at crisis management, both after there have been collisions between states (and there may be more, since states have reached—through transfers and through their own efforts—an incredibly higher level of armament that what existed only twenty years ago) and preventively. The second level of turmoil is the level of consensus; and here the key obstacle is the somewhat insuperable problem of ideology. There is no end of ideology in sight. One cannot even hope for what Henry Kissinger seemed to have expected, which is that states would freely practice their ideology at home, but refrain from exporting it or from acting upon its dictates outside, and thus behave abroad the way nonideological powers behave. States do not make this arbitrary distinction. A state that has a national ideology is going to try to spread it. What one can, however, ask for—and there will be no world order at all without it—is a reduction of the destructive external impact of those ideologies: an effort to bring down the level and to moderate the means of ideological competition. If the phrase had not already been invented, one could use the expression "peaceful coexistence"; or "nonviolent competition," if you like. There may be no way in which one can prevent ideology from being exported, but there are different ways of spreading ideas, and some are more murderous than others. One of the preconditions for that coexistence has to be a willingness to engage in discussion, dialog, communication with others even if we do not like their ideas. Finally, the third level has to do with the specific concrete cases of trouble in the world. Here, one has to go beyond crisis management and try to find better methods of conflict resolution; in the international economic realm one also should engage in serious negotiations and not just escapes, alibis, and procedural delays over the various grievances that we looked at in the last chapter.

The purpose of all these exhortations is not to abolish the international competition—it is here to stay—but simply to transform its character in two ways: first of all, by introducing considerations of long-term order into the ordinarily short-term calculations of statesmen—that is not easy because most statesmen do not have much time for long-term calculations, and often when they do theirs is a very parochial or very limited perspective, hence the permanent danger of self-serving hypocrisy. One can never expect another state to introduce such considerations unless one does it oneself; the rule of reciprocity is fundamental here. I have, previously, suggested some positive long-term considerations. There is an important negative one as well: the duty to prevent the unraveling of existing restraints. This means

that states should act in such a way as to prevent permanent enmity, as not to deny the humanity of the foe:
define your ends so as to make compatibility possible. It
also means something much less angelic: an obligation to
thwart the ends and means of others if their success
would make any return to moderation impossible. Finally, it means that one should never use methods that
make the return to moderation impossible.

The second way of trying to transform the international competition is by an increasing resort to collective forms of action. Self-reliance is not enough, and
confrontation is too dangerous. Again, there is a negative
implication, or precondition: statesmen should prevent
their own moral concerns from hardening into
ideologies. As we have seen in the last two chapters, even
while promoting their own values, they ought to search
for what is acceptable to the largest number of other
statesmen, even if the common denominator is low.
These are the precepts that aim at establishing, with and
through the states, a framework of order that will let
them play the game of international politics—but a game
whose nature will have changed profoundly.

To sum up, and this also points to the difference
between even the best kind of Machiavellian morality—
the morality of traditional, "realist" moderation—and
the morality of world order, we need a statecraft that
stresses long-term collective gains rather than short or
long-term national advantages; that accepts the need for
a large measure of institutionalization in international
affairs, and for important commitments of resources to
common enterprises; that shows great restraint in its use
of means; and that goes, in its choice of ends, far beyond
the realm of interstate relations.

The execution of such a design raises, of course,
many problems. The discussion that follows will concentrate on three structural problems and on two functional

ones, in addition to the three discussed in Chapters 2, 3, and 4. The three structural ones can be described in this way: if one looks at world order as a house (which is of course a perfectly arbitrary metaphor), the first question would be: "Can there be such a house at all?" The second one would be: "Who should build it?" And the third is: "What should it look like?" Should it look like the East Wing of the Washington National Gallery or like the Beaubourg Museum in Paris, if you like?

The first problem is that of feasibility, which has an extremely concrete name in contemporary international affairs. Whether there can be any world order at all depends on Soviet-American relations. Two opposite views exist in the literature, as well as in the political world. The first one is the "us vs. them" conception of international affairs, which comes in two forms. Both express the Machiavellian ethics, one in its more conflictual or confrontational form—the ethics of struggle and survival, the other in its more tempered, "rules of the game" version. The first form could be termed, "world order means winning the cold war": we will have world order once we have *prevailed;* victory is the precondition for a morally satisfactory form of world order. This is the *Commentary*-Moynihan-Senator Jackson-Ronald Reagan view of the world. The second variety could be defined as "world order as the central balance": We shall have world order as long as we *preserve* the equilibrium between us and them; that is the Kissinger conception, with its solid roots in traditional diplomatic history. The opposite position, which is the optimistic one, consists of saying that we can go ahead and build the house even without the Russians; it really doesn't matter. It too comes in two forms. The first (which cannot be found among statesmen, but only among academics) is the WOMP-ish or the Falk position. It consists of saying: "Let us do good, let us start building the house, and the ill humor, the resistance, and the evil intentions of the other side will just melt in the sunshine of our good example." Some years ago, there was another metaphor for this, the seesaw metaphor of the psychologist Charles Osgood: the superpowers are at the two ends of the seesaw, and the United States should take unilateral measures of restraint and disarmament, which would have us move along our side of the seesaw, and force the Soviets to move in the same direction, because otherwise they would lose balance. That is fine in seesaw terms, but you can question the relevance of the metaphor. The second form in which this optimistic view comes is the Carter administration version, vintage early 1977 (one always had to put a date); this essentially consists of the separation of two realms, and faith in our quality as the only full superpower. World order is specifically our business, undertaken with people who think like us—allies and Third World countries. The Soviets do not matter much because their only strong suit is the uniform. Economically, they are both weak and absent from the world scene. We have the whole panoply of assets. The only thing the Soviets can do is use military power, and insofar as this creates a peril for world order, we shall try to take care of it by a combination of collective Western self-reliance, and détente negotiations. Thus there are two different domains—that of East-West relations, functionally limited, and all the rest.

Both of these views, all four of these versions, are perfectly unacceptable. The first one, us vs. them, simply eliminates the moral problem. If everything that is anti-Soviet is ethical, there are really no more moral issues. All difficulties and troubles can be miraculously attributed to the enemy; one simply closes one's eyes to the imperfections of one's friends, and one subordinates the distribution of foreign aid to political conformity: assistance will go to those who are willing to be lined up with us—the Dulles view (except that Mr. Dulles never quite practiced what he preached). Those who oppose us, or act against our vested interests (as in Central America) can be seen as tools or as "objectively" the helpers of our enemy. Not only would this eliminate the moral problem, but it would aggravate practically all of our political ones: it is a perfect recipe for exacerbated arms races at every level, and it would turn most issues into East-West confrontations simply by misanalyzing them. By refusing to look at the local roots of internal and regional conflicts, by refusing to take seriously the economic grievances of Third World countries, it would make "prevailing" quite impossible, and could powerfully help the enemy's power and cause. The Kissinger view, which in its emphasis on balance rather than on victory and in its willingness to envisage arms control has the virtue of being less inflammatory, nevertheless shares that Manichaean misanalysis and falls into the contradiction of favoring at least covert interventions against the spread of "hostile" or radical regimes, while demanding of "them" that they cease exporting their kind of regime or supporting their clients abroad.

   The opposite view is also quite unrealistic but for different reasons. First, in many areas Soviet cooperation or participation is indispensable or essential, and we will not be able to obtain it entirely on our own terms. Furthermore, the Soviet Union's ability to spoil the construction — the Soviets' ability to remain our problem number one precisely because of the nature of their own ideology and ambitions—is quite enormous. Their choice when faced with the seesaw is simple: they can imitate us (which would be nice), or exploit our own moves to their advantage (which is less nice, but very tempting). I went to the Soviet Union just at the time when Mr. Carter explained that the fear of communism and, by implication, the problem of handling the Soviets, were no longer our main problem. They took it as a personal insult. They were determined to be our main headache.

As a result, the Soviet-American issue remains a global priority—and yet it cannot be allowed to become an obsession either. It is both a prerequisite and a centerpiece, the chief obstacle and the chief issue to work on. This is clearly where ethical and political considerations both converge and confront the most searing questions. After all, ethically, is not coexistence doubly repugnant, as many well-intentioned people argue? It is repugnant because of the nature of the Soviet regime; yet coexistence entails recognizing it. It is also repugnant because coexistence somehow ratifies not only the regime, but its conquests, and legitimizes its claims to be a kind of co-architect of world order with us. On the other hand, endless confrontation is extraordinarily dangerous—not only for all values in the world if we blow it up, but also for our own, because if the cold war becomes our only obsession we will end up looking and acting more and more like the enemy (watch already *Commentary* treating those who disagree with its view of the world as bad Americans, just as the Soviets treat dissidents as traitors). The logic of naïveté may lead us down a path not unlike the one Britain, France, and America followed in the 1930s, but the logic of confrontation leads either to another 1914, or to a garrison state in a world of total insecurity.

In this area, I see no alternative ethically and politically preferable to a highly complicated policy that tries to avoid opposite dangers by combining three factors. First, there must be firm opposition to aggression: outright aggression, and aggression through the technique which the Soviets seem to be developing with some virtuosity, as in Afghanistan, the technique of subversion and protective invasion—you install, by a coup, a "friendly" regime and then you explain that under the

Brezhnev doctrine you have a right to come to its defense. (This case should not be confused with the cases of Angola or Ethiopia, that is Soviet assistance to local leaders who may be clients but are not simple puppets installed by Moscow.) In that respect, what I discussed previously under the rubric of legitimate counter-intervention applies. The second element of the mix has to be preventive diplomacy (drying out the ponds so that the Soviets cannot fish in the gray areas, such as the Middle East, which present the greatest temptations for intrusion, hence the greatest dangers to peace). A third element, the most difficult to sell to the American public, is a new détente without illusions. We simply cannot expect the Soviets to embrace our notion of stability. They will keep playing their game; they will not play ours. Nevertheless we have to work on trying to limit both the intensity and the means with which they keep playing theirs. One way of doing this is to resume and expand negotiations on nuclear arms control; another is by attempting to maximize as often as possible convergent interests—in trade, in other kinds of exchanges, in crisis management, and in conflict resolution, for it is wrong to expect restrained Soviet behavior unless positive links and joint actions develop, which would give Moscow an incentive and, so to speak, a compensation for moderation: only a search for joint gains could slow the frantic quest for unilateral ones.[8] There is an enormous hubris, moral and political, in our trying to carry all the burdens ourselves; the world is full of problems which we simply cannot resolve alone and which the Soviet Union has the capacity to make worse or to keep from getting better, even when it has had nothing to do with their creation. This is extremely unsatisfying, morally, to people for whom East-West relations are a conflict between good and evil in which one side must win. And yet, if one remembers the imperative of self-restraint, the need to avoid the unravelling of those restraints which have already been built into the international system, and the duty to communicate, one must conclude that one has to try to move away from the pole of enmity, even if amity cannot be reached (it certainly cannot be reached by unilateral American smiles).

After asking "can there be a house at all," the second problem is the issue of leadership: "Who shall build it?" In the past, every international order has been a combination of two forms of leadership. One, in the areas of conflict and security, has been the collective leadership of the great powers (and that always led to disasters when the great powers split). In economic matters, normally, it has been the single leadership of one great power, which was laying down the rules (and there disaster came when that great power slipped, as England did at the end of the nineteenth and the beginning of the twentieth century, and no replacement came). At present, neither one of these two modes of leadership works. The society of great powers does not exist. The great powers do not particularly get along, and, above all, the old hierarchy, the old distinction between the great powers and the others, has been eroded—in part by nuclear weapons, in part by economic interdependence. As for economic leadership by one great power—in this case the United States—it worked for about twenty to twenty-five years, after the end of World War II. At present, a revolt against the rules laid down by the United States is being mounted by most of the new nations. The United States itself has changed the rules of the monetary game and is tampering with some of the commercial rules. America's own policies in the realms of money and oil, in the 60's and 70's, have contributed to the weakening of American power. Finally, there is a fragmentation of the international hierarchy—it is not the same depending on the issue one deals with.

The solutions to the problem of leadership are therefore extremely difficult. There is no possibility of a great power condominium. Even if we cannot avoid, sooner or later, cooperating with the Soviets on a number of issues (nuclear proliferation, food, oil, trade, a solution of the Arab-Israeli conflict, etc.) no condominium will do because neither the American public nor the other states will accept it. Another suggestion which has been made, with singular arrogance at times, is for us to simply go and co-opt some of the richer among the poor countries—some of the more advanced among the less developed countries. But most of them seem to have no particular interest in letting themselves be co-opted; their own power depends on their speaking for, or pretending to speak for, all the poor ones. Nor do they particularly want to be aligned with us; economically, they seek a revision of existing rules and regimes, not their mere inclusion in the old ones; politically, they want to remain themselves. Nor is it really in our interest, because it would be an extraordinarily unstable formula. This time, the solution will have to be messy—different leadership, different steering mechanisms depending on the functional problem, with all kinds of difficulties resulting from this. But even that could work only if the developed, richer states are willing to bear the costs of sharing their leadership in the hope of gaining long-term benefits in exchange; and if the undeveloped states, which will co-steer in many areas, behave not just as protesters, or as free riders, but as genuine participants: we are fairly far from this. Less monopolistic or oligarchic, and more diversified steering do not rule out acts of leadership, sometimes even unilateral acts, by a given state, as long as they are part of a strategy of collective action and management, and not mere attempts at hegemony or solitary play.

The third structural problem is the problem of

architecture. "What kind of house should this diverse crew try to build?" One has to build in two quite opposite directions. One, already mentioned, results from the need to move more toward cosmopolitanism. What it means in this particular instance is many more efforts at establishing and at consolidating international regimes, which are sets of rules and policies covering different issues and dealing both with procedures and with substance. Many such regimes exist already in economic realms; another one is being negotiated for the seas and oceans; they are also appropriate in the strategic-diplomatic domain, for instance for arms control and against nuclear proliferation. They have the great advantage of providing participating states both with restraints, and with opportunities for collective action. And they help insure the kind of coherence I have argued for, since they usually entail linked bargains and compromises, and patterned rather than improvised trade-offs.

More cosmopolitanism also means more steps toward collective management; this implies (even though they are rather unpopular in the United States at this time) a reinforcement of regional and international institutions, while recognizing that all of them, including the economic ones, are deeply political in their nature. Reinforcement does not mean proliferation or bureaucratic layering. It may well mean simplification, streamlining, and it surely means an increase in resources and powers. This is particularly important in two areas. The first one is the peace-keeping domain, where one has to make more of an effort at strengthening the very weak beginnings put in place by the United Nations, mainly in the 50's and early 60's. A machinery of observers and peace forces may become indispensable in a number of troubled situations where only the intervention of such forces could make possible a political solution that entails one state's retreat without loss of face, or a mutually acceptable policing of sensitive territories. The second area is the international economic domain, where one needs much greater collective management in two respects. One is the coordination of policies for mutual damage limitation (since states do a great deal of harm to each other, there have to be such collective measures on issues such as trade or credit policies or monetary fluctuations). The other task is the setting up of a new international economic order that will help the developed nations adjust beneficially to the profound structural changes in the world economy which result from the increased cost of energy, the enrichment of oil-exporting states, and the industrialization of other developing countries. This order should also help all the developing states promote their growth and meet the needs of their people. Establishing it will require, over time, a series of balanced deals, given, for instance, the connection between moderation in the pricing of oil and the establishment of a more stable international monetary system. Such deals are not conceivable without collective management and strong institutions.

This first direction entails centralization. But one has, at the same time, to work toward greater decentralization of the international system; one has to loosen the screws at two different levels. First, at the level of the states themselves, they need some degree of protection against excesses of interdependence. Interdependence becomes very rapidly unbearable, especially when it is not softened and made more acceptable by steady economic growth, which we have not had for several years, and especially when it is not made more bearable by smooth international steering, which also does not exist at present. States seem to be increasingly unwilling to bear the full costs of interdependence for external as well as for internal reasons.[9] The external reasons are fairly clear: interdependence means the constant manipulation of everybody by everybody, and it is made worse by the unevenness of power. The closer the bonds between states, the more insufferable inequality becomes. Inequality may be tolerable in the abstract, but when interdependence is tight, the weak will be constantly tempted to pull on the bonds in order to improve the deal they get from the strong, and the latter will be constantly challenged or even forced to share their wealth and their status. As for internal reasons, interdependence enhances the role of domestic interests, keen either on protection from abroad or on shifting burdens abroad. Also, the very fact that the functions of states have expanded as much as they have produces a violent reaction on the part of governments against constraints imposed from outside. This suggests two architectural lessons. First is the need to allow for a certain amount of loosening of the ties, a relative release of states from the burdens of uneven interdependence, a greater resort to self-reliant strategies to economic affairs. Secondly, there is a need for policies to reduce vulnerability—to limit external possibilities of blackmail.

This is not the only level in which one has to work for decentralization. There is also a level below the states. After all, many of the explosions which could rack the world are explosions within states, most of which are highly unstable. And those explosions would tempt foreign interventions. In many cases, there is considerable room for internal decentralization (but that would be the subject of another series of lectures). Whereas one cannot push the principle of self-determination so far that every Pimlico (to use the tale from a fine old English movie) becomes a sovereign state, there is leeway within most modern states for a margin of territorial and functional self-determination without full sovereignty. Many of them face acute problems of ethnic minorities, regional discontent, religious hostilities, cultural

separatisms, class conflicts, etc. It is when internal autonomy is suppressed or denied that demands for self-
determination escalate into claims of sovereignty, and
lead to the fragmentation of states. The somewhat utopian old nineteenth-century idea of *autogestion* which the
French socialists have picked up (and which is practically
the only useful thing they have picked up in recent years)
is an idea with a future. At either level the choice is
between some loosening and explosion.

The two functional problems I would like to
examine provide applications of the idea of coherence, of
interconnection of the parts. The first area is that of
armed conflict in the world. I have suggested some precepts about the actual use of force. But they are unlikely
to be followed in modern war conditions, as we know.
Moreover, this is only one part of the area. There is what
might be called a whole culture of force in interstate
relations: conventional arms sales, the export of nuclear
materials and technology that could be used to produce
weapons, a large number of unresolved conflicts—out of
all of which the actual resort to force might spring. This is
the realm where the interconnectedness of all foreign
policy issues is most obvious. Arms sales are very popular; advanced nations, and even states which are not that
advanced (Israel and several Latin American nations, for
instance), have become exporters of arms. Arms sales
and nuclear proliferation have a bright future as long as
states are insecure. States will be insecure as long as
fundamental disputes in which they are engaged have
not been resolved. Insecurity leads not only to classical
interstate violence, but to terrorism. And as long as the
disputes are not resolved and the armaments, nuclear or
conventional, increase, there will be not only violence,
but fewer funds available for development; and so on.
Everything is linked. And yet, once one has said this, one
also has to realize that statesmen face what has become

known, in the specialized literature, as the dove's dilemma. In other words, in order to prevent a country from going nuclear, should one not feed it conventional arms—an argument often made about Pakistan? If we do not want them to build *the* bomb, let us give them smaller bombs. Or if we want a country—say, Israel—to resolve a dispute, is not the best way of getting it in the proper mood, and of making it feel secure and strong enough to bargain, to feed it the weapons it needs? This has also been our recent justification with respect to arms sales to Morocco. Or else, is it not necessary, in the relations between the superpowers, to escalate the arms race so that we will get really balanced arms control agreements?

The answer I would give to this is, again, a complicated one. This is so, in the first place, because there is no room here for moral absolutism: it all depends on the situation; "disembodied morality always yields to complexity and caution once the nuts and bolts are brought onto the negotiating table, and moral *obiter dicta* usually recede into confusion once they are placed in a concrete context of cross-cutting allied, adversary and customer interests."[10] Secondly, often there is no dove's dilemma; the arguments that I have just outlined may turn out to be either false or entirely counterproductive: you will end up having both given conventional arms and incited a country to go nuclear, or you will, by giving it the weapons it wanted, have made it even more reluctant to offer concessions in order to solve the dispute at hand. And the more the arms race between the superpowers escalates, the more difficult further arms control becomes, the more fragile existing agreements (such as the ABM treaty of 1972) become. Thirdly, when there is a dove's dilemma, the yardstick should be fairly clear. The primary goal should be minimizing the risk of war. When there is a choice between alternative policies, all of which carry risks, one should choose the course that seems least likely to lead to war; between two courses that appear to entail approximately the same prospect of averting war, one ought to choose the one which, if war should come anyhow, is most capable of keeping it limited. The answer will vary from case to case. Sometimes the lesser peril may be to let a state go nuclear, rather than feeding it conventional weapons that would make a war much more likely; sometimes it will be the other way around.

Fourth, despite the occasional interrelation between the two courses, the proliferation of nuclear weapons and that of conventional weapons ought to remain distinct realms of policy. Even in those instances where the acquisition of a nuclear capability might not greatly increase the risks of war in an area, the problem of contagion and example is an important consideration. Here, there is a need for an international nonproliferation regime, given the limited effectiveness of individual restraint and sanctions. The aim of such a regime ought to be to strike a balance between legitimate transfers of technology essential or important for energy needs, and the imperative of preventing a process that could, in some areas such as the Middle East, or East Asia, or Southern Africa, aggravate insecurity, produce dangerous situations of mutual vulnerability, incite superpower interventions and reactions that could worsen the Soviet-American contest, and—should West Germany or Japan become nuclear powers—affect the central strategic balance.[11] Insofar as proliferation cannot be stopped, slowing down its rate and limiting its degree are important objectives. Collective leadership here is more frustrating than the exercise of unilateral preponderance—but even in the years of American preponderance proliferation did occur, and the alternative to an international regime is the kind of commercial and political competition that would only help the spread of nuclear weapons.

Fifth, with respect to conventional arms sales, it is indeed true that regional equilibrium (which may require them) is often more important than reductions *per se*; that the level of arms is often unrelated to war; that the sale of advanced technology may restore a balance when the weapons go to a state outnumbered by its opponent. But there is no guarantee that such a sale won't simply incite the opponent to look for similar weapons elsewhere—that is, that what was aimed at restoring balance won't lead to escalation; and while arms transfers are often caused by a situation's volatility, they can contribute to make it worse. The example of Iraq and Iran over the past ten years is clear. Obviously, unilateral restraints cannot achieve much, nor are they likely to survive the onslaught of domestic complaints in the selling country (when restraint leads to a competitor's windfall), or the pressure from the international contest; and collective restraint remains a distant dream. However, an ethical foreign policy ought not merely to practice "inconsistent restraint,"[12] but to follow certain guidelines: no sales of weapons clearly earmarked for aggression, or clearly helping the consolidation of a regime that violates human rights, or likely to lead (as did the Egyptian-Soviet arms deal of 1955) to an extension of the East-West contest or (arms sales to China might) to an intensification of that contest. Another guideline is to subordinate the sale to domestic improvements (South Korea) or to an effort to resolve the interstate conflict that triggered the sale (Middle East).

Finally, superpower arms control is an absolute duty, even if in the future agreements take different forms from the comprehensive treaties which have become technically monstrous and politically unmanageable. It is an absolute duty for all kinds of reasons. Technologically, if the arms race continues, we may reach a point where both sides will feel extremely vulnerable, or one side suspects that the other tries to reach a significant measure of superiority (by being able to strike at the bulk of the enemy's forces while protecting its own). This would be fatal for stability. We have been so used to nuclear stability that we find it hard to conceive that it may not be that way in ten or fifteen years at all. Arms control can help eliminate weapons that "would be wasteful, futile or particularly mischievous."[13] Also, as long as the superpowers keep increasing their nuclear arsenals, how can they demand from other states that they not build their own nuclear weapons? And yet we have to realize that there is a *de facto* linkage, between superpower arms control, the political structure of the Soviet-American contest, and the resolution of vital disputes in the world. I am not saying that we should make arms control dependent on the Soviets helping us resolve these disputes. But a world in which all major conflicts are unresolved is one in which it will be very difficult to sell arms control to the public and to the Congress.

The second functional problem which will be examined briefly is the problem of resource dependence, particularly with respect to oil. This is the realm where the interconnectedness between domestic issues and international issues is most obvious. The agenda of international relations is partly the same as the domestic economic agenda of states. In other words, there is a kind of escalation of the stakes of world politics: they have moved from the lofty and rarefied realm of honor and status, or from that of limited gains for special interests (as in the days of colonialism), to the bread and butter, jobs and pocketbook issues that are matters of life and death for most citizens. Also, with the loss of domestic control on instruments of policy, external processes and events have much more of an impact on domestic affairs (think of the impact of OPEC on the advanced economies, of the effect of monetary fluctuations on domestic currencies); and external processes are more necessary for domestic well being (think of aid and other resource transfers for poor countries, or of the need in which even the advanced economies find themselves to resort to summit meetings to prevent their economic policies from being completely out of phase). Finally, it is through international politics that one domestic political system can make an enormous imprint on another in economic matters.

The imperative, here again, is double. In the area of resources in particular, the first imperative is self-help. Domestic action is the beginning—only the beginning, yet the necessary beginning—of a solution. I have mentioned above reductions of vulnerability—making oneself less vulnerable to interdependence, to blackmail, to price *diktats*, or interruptions of supplies. This has to be done by domestic measures: anti-inflationary and anti-recessionary policies, adjustment assistance if trade becomes disruptive, and above all, in the realm of energy, measures of domestic conservation, stockpiling, diversification of energy sources, etc., rather than simply trying to keep prices one doesn't control from rising further without doing much to reduce one's dependence, or just lamenting how terrible it is to be dependent on unpredictable outside barbarians. But the second imperative is that these domestic measures must be taken in such a way as always to consider the effects they will have on others. If we look around us, there is very little reason for rejoicing. American economic policy in the mid-60's, under President Johnson, was perfectly irresponsible and largely caused the turmoil of the international monetary and economic system. The American attempt, in 1977, to force Bonn and Tokyo to follow our own "locomotive" policy of expansion, however well intentioned, was not much wiser. Worldwide inflation was at least partly fueled by U.S. policies. The long-term effect is what has to be watched, not the short-term benefit.

PERSONS

Let us now move from the lineaments of international order to the broader dimensions of world order. Ethics in international affairs is about the moral opportunities not only of states but of the people on whose behalf the states act. It is they who are both the frequent victims of world chaos, and the ultimate contributors to world order or disorder. I would like to present two sets of reflections, on cosmopolitanism, and on statecraft.

One condition of world order is the development of cosmospolitanism, by which I mean all transnational activities that do not carry a national label or cannot be reduced to their national components. A world of self-contained oases or self-contained islands in a state of siege is a very dangerous world. This does not mean that if there is cosmopolitan communication across borders there shall be peace—remember 1914 and what happened to the internationales of workers, business, or statesmen. But a world of closed units with little communication is a world with no room for mutual recognition and psychological deescalation in a crisis. One of our greatest present difficulties is that the transnational society which crosses borders and plays a vital role in economic affairs, communications, education, and science, as well as in the service of many good causes, does not coincide fully with the international system. One has to deal with the problem of the totalitarian powers. It is easy to be cosmopolitan in most of the noncommunist parts of the world, but not in the others. There is no way in which we—members of transnational groups that flourish—can act on this directly. Obviously, the closing off of the major communist states is partly a function of their international insecurity. However, their own state-of-siege mentality and measures contribute to and perpetuate this insecurity, and it has very often domestic roots in their own past, whether we think of China or of Russia. Also, the seige mentality may be necessary for the maintenance of their domestic power systems. Here, the only possibilities are oblique ones; the main hope lies in domestic evolution or crisis (a double-edged hope), and in the notion suggested above, which is not ideological disarmament—that is too much too soon—but a lowering of the intensity of ideological conflicts: ideological arms control. Even that is not going to work fast or with certainty. So for the time being we have to be resigned to the fact that cosmopolitanism will be possible only in some parts of the world. From an ethical point of view, this is both a source of weakness and a strength, since it means that in a large part of the world forces are at work that change the traditional picture of international politics as a game played by separate states (but beware of the nationalistic backlash too much cosmopolitanism can provoke).

In those parts of the world where it exists, cosmopolitanism—which comes in many forms—has to be amended from its present state in two radically different directions. There are two cosmopolitanisms I am concerned with here. The first one is that of the business managers, the multinational corporations, the private and public bankers, for instance. They need to adopt more resolutely an ethics of consequences. They must become more conscious of the fact that they are not, in the final analysis, anational, that they have a passport, or a flag, or a home country, and that their behavior abroad not only reflects back on their country but is often regarded as an expression of official policy by others, in the host countries or at the receiving end. They tend to see themselves as performing an essentially cosmopolitan function, but they do it from a very specific national base, very often an American one, and they are often not aware of the way this strikes others. Moreover, as we know, the root of their cosmopolitanism is not a dedication to humanity (this is a rationalization or—at best—an ultimate goal) but a concern for profit (the proximate goal); hence their way of jumping across borders, for tax or efficiency purposes, when there are too many local obstacles or when there is more to be gained by moving operations or transactions. They have to become much more concerned with the political and ethical effects of their acts on national policies. Otherwise, their brand of cosmopolitanism will trigger nationalist reactions. Paradoxically, what is needed on the part of the transnational managers is more national consciousness (I did not say nationalism, far from it, but awareness of the national phenomenon).

On the other hand, if we turn from the voluntary cosmopolitanism of capital to what I would call the forced cosmopolitanism of the driven and downtrodden—that of migrant labor and international refugees—what is needed here is almost the opposite; from victimized objects they have to become cosmopolitan subjects. I fear that both groups will continue to be a large and almost permanently refilled reservoir. The population explosion and the greater dynamism of the advanced economies are likely to keep driving the unemployed from poor countries, legally or illegally, into the developing ones. And as in Southeast Asia, or in Northwest Asia after the invasion of Afghanistan, domestic and regional turmoil will keep driving people out of their homes. In the case of the refugees, ethical action requires a cooperative effort of all but the poorest countries to rule out the degrading perpetuation of camps, and to provide for the resettlement of the refugees—who, in the past, have often contributed to the economic development of the countries that let them in. Should such an effort fail, it remains the duty of each country to open its own borders as widely as possible, without looking for excuses or waiting for others to act. Excuses and reasons for delay can always be found; and there may be real instances of "supreme necessity" limiting a nation's capacity to absorb refugees. A country suffering already from massive unemployment, or a state such as Malaysia, with an acute problem of ethnic heterogeneity, cannot be asked to undermine its social order by a policy of unrestricted access. And it is of course true that in a world in which the principle of nationality is the foundation of domestic and of international legitimacy, large numbers of refugees tend to dilute the national community which they join, and to be resented as alien intruders. But they deserve a chance to become part of this community. What is ethically imperative is an international, or failing that, a national guarantee not just of assistance but of settlement and integration in other countries.

In the case of the migrant workers, while the regulation of conditions of entry is likely to remain a domestic affair or a matter for bilateral negotiation rather than a subject of international rights and obligations, there is a moral duty of host states not simply to get rid of the foreign work force when a recession hits, nor to apply retroactive measures in order to thin its ranks. And while these workers are employed in the host country, they ought to be granted full equality of rights, except for the rights of political participation open only to nationals.

These are tall orders, amounting to a double revolution: a despecialization of the managers, and a lowering of barriers to help such easy victims as workers or refugees stop being pariahs. In order to get to this point, there are some preconditions. Three groups have an enormous responsibility in moving minds in those directions—intellectuals, the media, and educational systems, in the open parts of the world (there is no point in talking about the other parts). Where margins of freedom exist, these groups have moral duties. The duties of the intellectuals are exactly those that were defined by Camus. The role of the intellectual is not—as he angrily put it to Sartre, who never quite forgave him—to put himself and the armchair in which he sits in what he thinks is the direction of history; his duty is not to rationalize murder today because it might bring happiness tomorrow, to celebrate the purifying violence of today that ensures that the good shall win tomorrow. Quite simply his duty is to dismantle prejudices, national self-righteousness, and parochial views, patiently and painstakingly, to protest constantly against inequity and violence, which is not very easy; it is to be the conscience of national society. This carries two risks. One is the risk of pride (or vanity), the temptation to pontificate, to play God or guide; the other is the risk of becoming a victim of domestic witch hunts, since one cannot try to be a society's conscience without being its bad conscience at times. But if writers abdicate their responsibility, the intellectual world will become a mere arena for the domestics of power, or a mere battlefield between the leashed intellectuals in the totalitarian countries (or in all those countries where the intellectuals are in fact the valets of the state) and the voluntary justifiers of power and beaters of drums in the free countries. There is no necessary antagonism between truth and power, but there are tensions, and the intellectuals, if they have anything to learn from the experience of the twentieth century, ought to be at least on the side of truth, which is also the side of universality and reconciliation (but not appeasement of evil); it is also the side of limits on power.

The media, whether we think about the press or about television, also have important duties that they often fail to perform. One should not ask of them the equivalent of what the United Nations has sometimes asked of its members, which is that they reserve one percent of their GNP for foreign aid. We should not ask that the media reserve one percent of their time and space for the enlightenment of the public about realities in the outside world: that would be too arbitrary and probably too high a quota. But one could still ask that the balance between elucidation of the world and sheer entertainment be a bit less skewed, and one could also ask that whatever they do for elucidation be done without as much of a bent to oversimplify, without so much focusing on crises but not their origins, or on the picturesque or the exceptional. One could ask them to have a greater concern or respect for the sophistication of the public.

Finally, the educational system should be asked to move in two different directions. One is the cosmopolitan direction—away from the obsession with the history and culture and cult of the nation. There have been some mild attempts, in post-1945 western Europe, to push the curriculum away from a purely national focus. I am struck when I teach freshmen by how many of them have had fine courses in American history, and then one mish-mash known as "world history," of which there is not a single trace left. A more cosmopolitan education also requires, in this country, a major effort at teaching foreign languages. The other direction is that of despecialization, which is also a form of ethical training. Education ought to emphasize much more the interconnection of ethical and other issues. What one finds most of the time now is, on the one hand, disembodied ethical teaching, normally done by professional philosophers for specialists of philosophy. One example in this connection would be the journal *Philosophy and Public Affairs,* in which one often finds political issues discussed with beautiful logic but without reference to the political universe. On the other side of the barricade there is the teaching of techniques, nuts and bolts, sometimes called "methodologies," without awareness that much of any subject worth studying deals with problems which are at

least partly issues of ethical choice. In other words, despecialization would help bury the exaggerations that
have bloated the old distinctions between facts and values, or between what is supposedly scientific and what is
supposedly subjective.

If one puts together these remarks about the intellectuals, the media, and education, they amount to one
thing—a demand that they adopt a critical perspective,
without being at all intimidated by the philistine fear that
if one is too critical toward one's own system, one thereby
gives an advantage to *the* enemy. On the contrary. There
is a difference, of course, between a critical perspective
for reform or for the discarding of national blinders, and
systematic denigration for destruction. The latter is, in
fact, quite rare. The former is a precondition for ethical
action, a guarantee against self-righteousness or hypocrisy, and an asset that totalitarian powers destroy or waste
to their peril.

What about the average citizens? It is difficult for
them to find the right balance between cosmopolitanism
and nationalism—the modern state is the framework of
their lives, the target of their hopes and resentments, and
the outside world is either a field for the relaxation of
tourism—a spectacle, or a source of economic disrup-
tions and violent conflicts—a threat. I have in Chapter 2
discussed briefly the wartime dilemmas and duties of the
citizens of free countries. In peacetime, they have a double obligation. One is to forget neither the state's legitimate concerns with survival and security, nor the fact that
world order itself requires resistance to aggression and
a dismissal of appeasement. The attitude expressed in
the 1930s by a French labor leader who stated his preference for servitude over war, since one can climb out of the
former but not recover from death on the battlefield, is
lamentable, unless one is an absolute pacifist. But the
other duty is to overcome chauvinism and to work as

much as one can for world order: to push one's government in the right directions—arms control, policies of distributive justice, fairness to refugees or foreigners; to keep it away from the tinsel Machiavellianism that prostitutes the notion of national security in order to justify shabby or deluded external interventions and shady or vindictive domestic persecutions; to substitute for or to supplement the government in areas where interstate politics is stymied but citizens can have influence, as in the realm of human rights. How much can citizens actually accomplish? At a minimum, they can vote, which of course many Americans don't do (always a source of great surprise to non-Americans, for whom the conquest of the right to vote took a few centuries). They can, by their pressures on their representatives or by their own efforts, affect at least some things; and the smaller the community or the tighter it is, the more of a chance they have to affect things.

This leaves one category of persons about whom a few last remarks are necessary: statesmen. If one thinks about world order, just as incrementalism and traditional moderation are not enough, classical statecraft is deficient. Traditional statecraft is made of three types of people. First is the crusader statesman, whether he sees himself simply as the secular arm of a great cause or whether he is in fact a national expansionist, advancing behind an ideological shield. The crusader has become too dangerous to bear. Premature idealism can lead to disasters (moral conviction, after all, is not enough); this may not be, in fact, a very great danger, for there are very few statesmen who are that rashly idealistic. The more likely danger—well displayed in this century—is that of cynicism and brutality. The second traditional type is the hero-statesman, the heroic leader *à la* Churchill or De Gaulle. These are statesmen endowed with quite extraordinary virtues as national providers. They are great leaders in periods of distress. Yet their role is to emphasize the particular mission of their nation; this means either that they do not stress sufficiently the cooperative dimension international relations must have (remember De Gaulle's methods within the European Community), or that they do not understand or do not sympathize with the cosmopolitan one. They are suspicious of those two dimensions because they are always afraid that their nation will be manipulated.

The third type, the most usual, is the conservative statesman, of whom, in many respects, the best recent example was Henry Kissinger. One cannot deny— certainly he would not—that he had a moral purpose: interstate order through the balance of power and the dampening of conflicts. But conservative statecraft has had extraordinary shortcomings. First, it is an "engineering" conception of statecraft. Order must have a content beyond equilibrium, otherwise it becomes pure mechanics. Equilibrium is an ingredient or a precondition, not an inspiration or a vision. Also, it has always had an extraordinary "great power" aspect. The lesser breeds are subordinated to the concerns of the big ones, as Kissinger's treatment of some of the lesser breeds showed (he writes in his book that Cambodia was not a moral issue, it was a tactical choice[14]). The last shortcoming has to do with the problems of means and consequences. The conservative statesman always believes that relying on force—intervention, subversion, deception—is perfectly proper, and that again has its dangers at home and abroad.

What one needs, and what one does not find much of, is a transcendence of past types of statecraft. The best that we seem to be able to get at present is the pragmatic manager, whose great virtue is trouble-avoidance (but remember that most of the statesmen who were in power in the summer of 1914 were pragmatic managers, starting with Bethmann-Hollweg). As President Jimmy Carter often displayed an almost schizophrenic disconnection between lofty principles and daily tactics with no strategy in between. Obviously, one needs statesmen who will continue to manage the national interest and to promote the prestige and power of their nations in the world, because that is what they are there for. A statesman is not chosen simply to promote disembodied universal moral concepts. But one also needs two extra dimensions. One, mentioned earlier, is the capacity to think about the long term. This is particularly difficult in modern states, where the combination of mobilized interests, complex issues, bureaucratic ponderousness, and electoral deadlines, relentlessly pushes the short term on top. But here institutions can make a difference, and the institutions of the United States, as they are at present, almost make it impossible for the president to concentrate on the long term. Also needed, even in a world still divided into nations, is a capacity to rise beyond the purely national. It is true, as Wolfers put it, that "a single powerful government (he was thinking, of course, of the Soviet Union, and of prewar Nazi Germany) engaged, for whatever reasons, in a policy of aggression and aggrandizement may force all others into line with its Machiavellian practices, provided these others have the will to survive."[15] But one has to remember that even when survival is at stake, or vital security interests, there is always a choice: the purely short-term nationalistic response is not necessarily the wise one; also, the higher purpose of statecraft is to act in such a way that High Noon situations between great powers do not occur too often—and that when they occur, there can be other acceptable solutions than a shoot-out.

In an earlier chapter, the problem of international politics was defined as turning a vicious circle into a spiral; I have no illusions about it being achievable or achieved in the near future. But "it is not necessary to hope in order to undertake, or to succeed in order to persevere."

Notes

1—ETHICS AND INTERNATIONAL AFFAIRS

1. Michael Walzer, *Just and Unjust Wars* (New York: Basic Books, 1977).
2. John Rawls, *A Theory of Justice* (Cambridge, Mass.: Harvard University Press, 1971), p. 19.
3. Thucydides, *The Peloponnesian War* (New York: Modern Library, 1934), p. 334.
4. Robert W. Tucker in Robert E. Osgood and Robert W. Tucker, *Force, Order and Justice* (Baltimore: Johns Hopkins University Press, 1967), Part 2, Chapter 3.
5. It is admirably analyzed by Raymond Aron in *Max Weber and Sociology Today*, ed. Otto Stammer (New York: Harper, 1971), pp. 83–101, originally published as "Max Weber et la politique de puissance," *Preuves* (November 1964).
6. See my essay, "Rousseau on War and Peace," in *The State of War* (New York: Praeger, 1965).
7. In what remains the best essay on our subject: "Statesmanship and Moral Choice," in *Discord – Collaboration* (Baltimore: Johns Hopkins University Press, 1965), p. 62.
8. Quoted by Arthur Schlesinger in *Ethics and World Politics: Four Perspectives*, ed. Ernest W. Lefever (Baltimore: Johns Hopkins University Press, 1972).
9. Niccolò Machiavelli, *Discourses* (New York: Modern Library, 1950), Part 3, Chapter 41, p. 528.
10. Quoted by J. B. D. Miller, "Morality, Interests and

Rationalization," in *Moral Claims in World Affairs*, ed. Ralph Pettman (London: Croom Helm, 1979), p. 42.

11. Immanuel Kant, *The Philosophy of Kant* (New York: Modern Library, 1949), p. 459.

12. See a contrary argument in Charles R. Beitz, *Political Theory and International Relations* (Princeton: Princeton University Press, 1979), passim. See also, for a defense of self-determination, Dov Ronen, *The Quest for Self-Determination* (New Haven, Conn.: Yale University Press, 1979).

13. Bernard Williams, *Morality* (New York: Harper, 1972), p. 23.

14. Beitz, *Political Theory*, p. 65.

15. Williams, *Morality*, pp. 76–77. A contrario, Beitz, *Political Theory*, pp. 56–58.

16. Sissela Bok, *Lying* (New York: Vintage Books, 1978), p. 53.

2—THE USE OF FORCE

1. The most exhaustive (and exhausting) analysis is to be found in E. B. F. Midgley, *The Natural Law Tradition and the Theory of International Relations* (New York: Barnes and Noble, 1975). See also Frederick O. Bonkovsky, *International Norms and National Policy* (Grand Rapids, Mich.: Eedmans, 1980).

2. The following section develops ideas presented more sketchily in the author's *Primacy or World Order* (New York: McGraw Hill, 1978), pp. 163–64.

3. Robert W. Tucker, *The Just War* (Baltimore: Johns Hopkins University Press, 1960), p. 199.

4. Robert E. Osgood and Robert W. Tucker, *Force, Order and Justice* (Baltimore, Johns Hopkins University Press, 1967), pp. 311–13.

5. In his enormous book, *The Just War* (New York: Scribners, 1968), Paul Ramsey, who seeks to make just war possible, does not address himself to the problem of ends.

6. Charles R. Beitz, *Political Theory and International Relations* (Princeton: Princeton University Press, 1979), pp. 51–53.

7. Michael Walzer, *Just and Unjust Wars*, (New York: Basic Books, 1977), pp. 58–59.

8. Bonkovsky, *International Norms*, p. 45.

9. See my analysis in "International Law and the Control of Force," in *The Relevance of International Law*, ed. Karl Deutsch and Stanley Hoffmann (New York: Doubleday Anchor, 1971), pp. 44–47.

10. Ibid., p. 85.

11. Michael Walzer, "The Moral Standing of States," *Philosophy and Public Affairs* 9, no. 3 (Spring 1980): 218–19.

12. I disagree with David Luban who, in "Just War and Human Rights," *Philosophy and Public Affairs* 9, no. 2 (Winter 1979): 167ff., writes that "only the vertical contract can legitimate a state." There is nothing contractual about the foundation of a people or a nation; there is about that of a state.

13. Beitz, *Political Theory*, pp. 83ff., 103–104, 105–115.

14. Gerald Doppelt, "Walzer's Theory of Morality in International Relations," *Philosophy and Public Affairs* (Fall 1978), pp. 13ff.

15. Ibid., p. 217 n11.

16. Ibid., p. 226.

17. R. J. Vincent, "Western Conceptions of a Universal Moral Order," *British Journal of International Studies* 4 (1978): 43. See also his book, *Non-Intervention and International Order* (Princeton: Princeton University Press, 1974), Chapter 9.

18. Walzer, *Just and Unjust Wars*, p. 99.

19. See Robert Jervis, "Why Nuclear Superiority Does Not Matter," *Political Science Quarterly* 94, no. 4 (Winter 1979–80): 617–34.

20. Michael Walzer, *Obligations* (Cambridge, Mass.: Harvard University Press, 1970), p. 224.

21. Thomas Nagel, "War and Massacre," *Philosophy and Public Affairs* 1 and 2 (Winter 1972): 132.

22. R. B. Brandt, "Utilitarianism and the Rules of War," *Philosophy and Public Affairs* 1 and 2 (Winter 1972): 157. See Jonathan Glover's commentary in *Causing Death and Saving Lives* (New York: Penguin, 1977), pp. 273ff.

23. Walzer, *Just and Unjust Wars*, p. 230.

24. Ibid., p. 146.

25. In a forthcoming Adelphi Paper (London: International Institute for Strategic Studies).

26. One currently discussed way of deterring counterforce nuclear war is a revival of ballistic missile defenses aimed at protecting land-based missile sites, should technology make effective defense possible. However, there are three caveats. Other military targets could become even more attractive. An attempt by one superpower to deploy such ABM ahead of its rival, while increasing its own ability to strike the adversary's land-based missiles, would be highly destabilizing. And an abandonment of the anti-ABM treaty of 1972, at a time when SALT process is in very serious trouble, would reduce strategic arms control to very little, and probably induce each superpower to find ways of restoring the advantage for the offense (just as the fear of an effective Soviet ABM system, a dozen years ago, triggered the development of MIRV by the U.S.).

27. Some of what follows is borrowed from "War Crimes: Political and Legal Issues," *Dissent* (December 1971), pp. 530–34.

28. For an intelligent philosophico-legal attempt at dealing with many of the issues discussed in this chapter, see Yehuda Melzer, *Concepts of Just War* (Leyden: A. W. Sijthoff, 1975).

3—THE PROMOTION OF HUMAN RIGHTS

1. See Hedley Bull's chapter in *Moral Claims in World Affairs*, ed. Ralph Pettman (London: Croom Helm, 1979).

2. George Kennan, quoted by Kenneth Thompson, "New Reflections on Ethics and Foreign Policy: The Problem of Human Rights," *Journal of Politics* 40, no. 4 (November 1978): 993.

3. Maurice Cranston, "What are Human Rights," in *The Human Rights Reader*, ed. Walter Laqueur and Barry Rubin (New York: New American Library, 1979), pp. 17–24.

4. Ronald Dworkin, *Taking Rights Seriously* (Cambridge, Mass.: Harvard University Press, 1978), p. 92.

5. Thomas Scanlon, "Human Rights as a Neutral Concern," in *Human Rights and U.S. Foreign Policy*, ed. Peter G. Brown

and Douglas MacLean (Lexington: Lexington Books, 1978), pp. 83–92.

6. Julian R. Friedman, "The Meaning of Human Rights," unpublished paper, 1977, p.10.

7. Charles Beitz in Brown and MacLean, *Human Rights*, p. 59.

8. Charles Frankel, *Human Rights and Foreign Policy*, Headline Series 241 (New York: Foreign Policy Association, October 1978), Chapter 5.

9. Rita E. Hauser, "A First World View," in *Human Rights and American Foreign Policy*, ed. Donald P. Kommers and Gilbert D. Loescher (Notre Dame: University of Notre Dame Press, 1978), pp. 85–89.

10. Henry Shue in Brown and MacLean, *Human Rights*, pp. 75ff.

11. Sandy Vogelgesang, *American Dream/Global Nightmare* (New York: Norton, 1980), p. 192.

12. Ibid. p. 197. See also the discussion of the relation between the satisfaction of human needs and political rights in Tom J. Farer, *Towards a Humanitarian Diplomacy: A Primer for Policy* (New York: New York University Press, forthcoming).

13. George Kennan, *The Cloud of Danger* (Boston: Little, Brown, 1977), pp. 38–39.

14. See the remarks by Marcel Gauchet, "Les droits de l'homme ne sont pas une politique," *Le Débat* (July–August 1980), pp. 13ff.

15. Herbert C. Kelman, "The Conditions, Criteria and Dialectics of Human Dignity," *International Studies Quarterly* 21, no. 3 (September 1977): 543.

16. For a detailed survey see Myres S. McDougal, Harold Lasswell, and Lung-Chu Chen, *Human Rights and World Public Order* (New Haven, Conn.: Yale University Press, 1980), unfortunately embedded in the two senior authors' familiar scholasticism. For a briefer survey see A. H. Robertson in Kommers and Lescher, *Human Rights*, pp. 5–31.

17. Peter G. Brown in Brown and MacLean, *Human Rights*, p. 168.

18. Bryce Wood in Jorge Dominguez et al., *Enhancing Global Human Rights* (New York: McGraw Hill, 1979), p. 194.

19. Dominguez, *Enhancing Global Human Rights,* p. 45.

20. Ernst B. Haas, *Global Evangelism Rides Again,* Institute of International Studies Policy Paper in International Affairs no. 5 (Berkeley: Unversity of California, 1978), pp. 30ff.

21. OAS, LACHR, "Report on the Situation of Human Rights in Argentina" (April 1980), pp. 26–27.

22. Vogelgesang, *American Dream,* p. 251.

23. William F. Buckley, Jr., "Human Rights and Foreign Policy," *Foreign Affairs* (Spring 1980), pp. 775–96.

24. Stanley Hoffmann, *Primacy or World Order* (New York: McGraw Hill, 1978), p. 322.

25. In Laqueur and Rubin, *Human Rights Reader,* pp. 25ff.

26. Richard M. Nixon, *The Real War* (New York: Warner Books, 1980), p. 272.

27. Report of the National Policy Panel of the UN Associations of the USA, *United States and Human Rights* (December 1979).

28. Ibid., pp. 174, 222.

29. Arthur Schlesinger, "Human Rights and the American Tradition," *Foreign Affairs: America and the World 1978,* pp. 518ff.

30. In addition to Vogelgesang, see Thomas M. Frank and Edward Weisband, *Foreign Policy by Congress* (New York: Oxford University Press, 1979), 84ff.

31. In Dominguez, *Enhancing Global Human Rights,* pp. 186ff.

32. See Rupert Emerson, "The Fate of Human Rights in the Third World," *World Politics* 27, no. 2 (January 1975): 201–226.

33. See Charles William Maynes and Richard H. Ullman, "Ten Years of Foreign Policy," *Foreign Policy,* no. 40 (Fall 1980), p. 8.

34. The case of Ethiopia turning to the USSR in 1977 is different. First, the original American decision to reject the new Ethiopian regime's request for arms was made by Kissinger, not, of course, on human rights grounds. And the Carter decision to vote against multilateral loans to Ethiopia on such grounds in early 1977 may have been mistaken, given the new regime's efforts in the realm of economic and social rights (it was politically repressive, but

its predecessor—our client—has been both repressive and
rather indifferent to economic and social rights).
35. See Irving R. Kaufman, "A Legal Remedy to International
Torture," *New York Times Magazine*, November 9, 1980,
pp. 44ff.
36. See Tom Harkin, "Human Rights and Foreign Aid," in
Brown and MacLean, *Human Rights*, pp. 15–26.
37. For a discussion of the issues see the articles by Robert I.
Rotberg, Desaix Myers III and David M. Liff, and Randall
Robinson in *Foreign Policy* 38 (Summer 1980). See also
Andrew Nagorski, "U.S. Solutions vis-à-vis South Africa,"
in Jennifer Whitaker, *Africa and the U.S.* (New York: New
York University Press, 1978). For a proposal that is both
tough and thoughtful see Clyde Ferguson and William
Cotter, "South Africa: What is to be Done," *Foreign Affairs*
(January 1978), pp. 253–74.
38. Ferguson and Cotter, "South Africa," pp. 525–26.
39. William Shawcross, *Sideshow* (New York: Simon and
Schuster, 1979).
40. In Dominguez, *Enhancing Global Human Rights*, pp. 207–
257.

4—PROBLEMS OF DISTRIBUTIVE JUSTICE

1. John Rawls, *A Theory of Justice* (Cambridge, Mass.: Harvard University Press, 1971), p. 5.
2. For other kinds of justice see Hedley Bull, *The Anarchical
Society* (New York: Columbia University Press, 1977),
Chapter 4.
3. See the excellent account by Robert L. Rothstein, *The Weak
in the World of the Strong* (New York: Columbia University
Press, 1977).
4. "Approaches to the Notion of International Justice," in
The Future of the International Legal Order, ed. Cyril Black
and Richard Falk (Princeton: Princeton University Press)
I: 409.
5. Robert W. Tucker, *The Inequality of Nations* (New York:
Basic Books, 1977).

6. Fouad Ajami, "The Global Logic of the Neoconservatives," *World Politics* 30, no. 3 (April 1978): 462.

7. See remarks by Albert Bressand, "Six dialogues en quête d'auteur," *Politique Etrangère* (June 1980), pp. 308ff.

8. Nathaniel H. Leff, "Changes in the American Climate Affecting the NIEO Proposals," *The World Economy* (1979), p. 96.

9. In "Equity in the South in the Context of North-South Relations," in Albert Fishlow et al., *Rich and Poor Nations in the World Economy* (New York: McGraw Hill, 1978), pp. 173ff.

10. In Jagdish N. Bhagwati, ed., *The New International Economic Order: The North-South Debate* (Cambridge, Mass.: MIT Press, 1977), p. 355.

11. Ibid., pp. 94ff.

12. See Samuel Gorowitz, "Bigotry, Loyalty and Malnutrition," in *Food Policy*, ed. Peter G. Brown and Henry Shue (New York: Free Press, 1977), p. 136.

13. Theodore Sumberg, *Foreign Aid as Moral Obligation?* The Washington Papers no. 10 (Beverly Hills, Calif.: Sage, 1973).

14. Ibid., p. 154.

15. Charles R. Beitz, "Bounded Morality," *International Organization* 33, no. 3 (Summer 1979): 421.

16. Gorowitz, "Bigotry, Loyalty and Malnutrition," p. 141.

17. Charles R. Beitz, *Political Theory and International Relations* (Princeton: Princeton University Press, 1979), p. 141.

18. Robert Amdur, "Rawls' Theory of Justice," *World Politics* 29, no. 3 (April 1977): 452ff.

19. W. H. Smith, "Justice: National, International or Global," in *Moral Claims in World Affairs*, ed. Ralph Pettman (London: Croom Helm, 1979), p. 105.

20. Beitz, "Bounded Morality," p. 421.

21. Tony Smith, "The Underdevelopment of Development Literature," *World Politics* 21, no. 2 (January 1979): 247–88.

22. Richard Cooper, "A New International Economic Order for Mutual Gain," *Foreign Policy*, no. 26 (Spring 1977), pp. 87ff.

23. Johan Galtung, *The True Worlds* (New York: Free Press, 1980), pp. 113ff.

24. James Caporaso, "Methodological Issues in the Measurement of Inequality, Dependence and Exploitation," in Steven J. Rosen and James R. Kurth, *Testing Theories of Economic Imperialism* (Lexington: Lexington Books, 1974), pp. 108–110.

25. Willy Brandt et al., *North-South* (Cambridge, Mass.: MIT Press, 1980).

26. Cf. C. Fred Bergsten, "The Threat from the Third World," *Foreign Policy* 2 (Summer 1973): 102–124.

27. Harry G. Johnson in Bhagwati, *New International Economic Order*, p. 360.

28. Quoted in Roger Hansen, *Beyond the North-South Stalemate* (New York: McGraw Hill, 1979), p. 61.

29. Cf. Thomas Nagel, "Poverty and Food: Why Charity is Not Enough," in Brown and Shue, *Food Policy*, pp. 54ff.

30. Keith Griffin, *International Inequality and National Poverty* (New York: Macmillan, 1978).

31. See Alfred Maizels, "A New International Strategy for Primary Commodities," in *A World Divided*, ed. G. K. Helleiner (Cambridge, Mass.: Cambridge University Press, 1976), pp. 33ff.

32. Mahbub ul Haq, *The Poverty Curtain* (New York: Columbia University Press, 1976), pp. 158–59.

33. Cf. Gunnar Adler-Karlsson, "Eliminating Absolute Poverty," in W. Howard Wriggins and Adler-Karlsson, *Reducing Global Inequalities* (New York: McGraw Hill, 1978), pp. 158ff.

34. See for instance André Gunder Frank and Samir Amin, "Self-Reliance and the New International Economic Order," *Monthly Review* 29, no. 3 (July/August 1977): 1–21.

35. The best review of all the versions is by Robert W. Cox, "Ideologies and the New International Economic Order," *International Organization* 33, no. 2 (Spring 1979): 257–302.

36. Albert Fishlow, "A New International Economic Order," in Fishlow et al., *Rich and Poor Nations in the World Economy* (New York: McGraw Hill, 1978), p. 41.

37. Arthur Lewis, *The Evolution of the International Economic Order* (Princeton: Princeton University Press, 1978).

38. Ibid., p. 14.

39. Thomas Biersteker, "Self-Reliance in Theory and Practice in Tanzania Trade Relations," *International Order* 34, no. 2 (Spring 1980): 229–64.

40. Richard Fagen, "A Funny Thing Happened on the Way to the Market," *International Organization* 32, no. 1 (Winter 1978): 291.

41. Fouad Ajami, *Human Rights and World Order Policies*, World Orders Model Project Working Paper no. 4 (New York: 1978), p. 31.

42. Frances Stewart, "The Direction of International Trade," in Helleiner, *A World Divided*, p. 95.

43. See the remarks by Richard Cooper, "New International Economic Order," pp. 93ff, and Rachel McCulloch and José Pinera, "Alternative Community Trade Regimes," in Ruth W. Arad et al., *Sharing Global Resources* (New York: McGraw Hill, 1979), p. 115.

44. Cf. Catherine Gwin in Wriggins, *Reducing Global Inequalities*, p. 13.

45. Miriam Camps, *The Case for a New Global Trade Organization* (Council on Foreign Relations, 1980), pp. 8–9.

46. The RIO (Reshaping the International Order) Report to the Club of Rome, coordinated by Jan Tinbergen (New York: Dutton, 1976) is particularly prolific in its suggestions for new international agencies.

47. Joan E. Spero, *The Politics of International Economic Relations* (New York: St. Martin's, 1977), pp. 141ff.

48. Cox, "Ideologies," pp. 282–83.

49. Carlos Diaz-Alejandro, "Delinking North and South," in Fishlow, *Rich and Poor Nations*, pp. 154–55. See also Roger D. Hansen, "North-South Policy—What is the Problem," *Foreign Affairs* 58, no. 5 (Summer 1980): 1104–128.

50. Rothstein, *Weak in the World*, p. 350.

51. Diaz-Alejandro, "Delinking North and South," p. 159.

52. James P. Grant, "Development: The End of Trickle Down?" *Foreign Policy* 12 (Fall 1973): 60.

53. For the analysis of this power, see Albert O. Hirshman,

"Beyond Asymmetry," *International Organization* 32, no. 1 (Winter 1978): 45–50, and Theodore H. Moran, "Multinational Corporations and Dependency," pp. 79–100.

54. Mahbub ul Haq, "Negotiating the Future," *Foreign Affairs* 59, no. 2 (Winter 1980–81): 408–409.

55. I have also learned much from an excellent unpublished paper by Michael Doyle, "The New International Economic Order: Genesis and Prognosis," 1980.

56. In Bhagwati, *New International Economic Order*, p. 371.

57. Cf. Richard Cooper's formulations: the transferred benefits should "benefit those residents of the recipient countries who are clearly worse off than the worst-off 'taxed' residents of the donor countries," in Bhagwati, *New International Economic Order*, p. 356.

58. Cf. Reginald H. Green, "Aspects of the World Monetary and Resource Transfer System in 1974," in Helleiner, *A World Divided*, pp. 265ff.

59. Ibid., p. 71.

60. Cf. Henry Shue, "Distributive Criteria for Development Assistance," in Brown and Shue, *Food Policy*, pp. 305–318. He resolves all the uncertainties by advocating the best of all (alternative) solutions simultaneously.

61. Ibid., p. 291.

62. See the remarks of Sandy Vogelgesang, *American Dream/ Global Nightmare* (New York: Norton, 1980), p. 203.

63. *Memoires of Hope* (New York: Simon and Schuster, 1971), p. 162.

5—AN ETHICS OF WORLD ORDER

1. Arnold Wolfers, *Discord and Collaboration* (Baltimore: Johns Hopkins University Press, 1965), p. 64.

2. Hedley Bull, *The Anarchical Society* (New York: Columbia University Press, 1977), p. 20.

3. Robert C. Johansen, *The National Interest and the Human Interest* (Princeton: Princeton University Press, 1980), p. 306.

4. Johan Galtung, *The True Worlds* (New York: Free Press, 1980), see especially pp. 87–94.

5. Rajni Kothari, *Footsteps into the Future* (New York: Free Press, 1974), p. 13, Chapter 5.

6. Stanley Hoffmann, *Primacy or World Order* (New York: McGraw Hill, 1978).

7. James Akins, in *Foreign Affairs* 51, no. 3 (April 1973): 462–90.

8. For further elaboration see "Muscle and Brains," *Foreign Policy* 37 (Winter 1979–80): 3–27. See also Robert Legrold, "Containment without Confrontation," *Foreign Policy* 40 (Fall 1980): 74–98.

9. For further elaboration see "Domestic Politics and Interdependence," in *From Marshall Plan to Global Interdependence* (Paris: OECD, 1978), pp. 181–201.

10. Richard Betts, "The Tragicomedy of Arms Trade Control," *International Security*, no. 5, pt. 1 (Summer 1980): 106.

11. See Joseph Nye, "Maintaining a Non-Proliferation Regime," *International Organization* (Winter 1980–81).

12. Betts, "Tragicomedy of Arms Trade Control," p. 94. On the previous arguments see pp. 80–95.

13. George Rathjens and Jack Ruina, "Nuclear Doctrine and Rationality," *Daedalus* 110, no. 1 (Winter 1981), p. 187.

14. Henry Kissinger, *White House Years* (Boston: Little, Brown, 1979), p. 515.

15. Ibid., p. 64.

Index

DUTIES BEYOND BORDERS

was composed in 11-point Baskerville VIP and leaded two points
by Utica Typesetting Company, Inc.;
with display type in Baskerville Monotype and Foundry
by J. M. Bundscho Inc.;
printed by sheet-fed offset on 60-pound acid-free Warren Old Style Wove,
Smyth-sewn and bound over boards in Holliston Crown Linen,
also adhesive bound with 10-point Carolina laminated covers,
by Maple-Vail Book Manufacturing Group, Inc.;
and published by

SYRACUSE UNIVERSITY PRESS

Syracuse, New York 13244-5160